CHASING THE DRAGON

CHASING THE DRAGON
Will India Catch Up with China?

MOHAN GURUSWAMY
ZORAWAR DAULET SINGH

Longman
is an imprint of

PEARSON

Delhi • Chennai • Chandigarh

ISBN 978-81-317-2411-8

10 9 8 7 6 5 4 3

Published by Dorling Kindersley (India) Pvt. Ltd., licensees of Pearson Education in South Asia.

Head Office: 7th Floor, Knowledge Boulevard, A-8(A), Sector-62, Noida 201309, UP, India.
Registered Office: 14 Local Shopping Centre, Panchsheel Park, New Delhi 110 017, India.

Typeset by Integra Software Solutions

Printed in India by Swan Press

CONTENTS

LIST OF CHARTS

LIST OF TABLES

PREFACE

In late 2003, in the wake of the high-decibel 'India Shining' campaign by the Government of India, the Centre for Policy Alternatives began a comparison of the post-reform economic performances of China and India. Even the initial cursory study of basic macroeconomic data was quite revealing. After entering the mid-1970s with a much lower per capita income than India, China had begun to leave it far behind in the 1980s. All through the 1990s, this gap only began to widen. It was only in the first years of the new millennium that India's economic growth had begun to look somewhat optimistic, though still not anywhere close to that of China's. Nevertheless, while India seemed shining for some, little had changed for decades for the overwhelming majority. Thus, we published our first paper 'Will India Catch-up with China?' (Mohan Guruswamy and Abhishek Kaul) and sent it to all Members of Parliament and senior players in the policy- and opinion-making circles, with a covering letter from the late Chandrashekhar, former Prime Minister.

The response was quite stunning. Those in the government, like the then Foreign Minister, unable to dispute hard facts, wrote quibbling over the lack of democracy in China and India's 'system' as causes for its tardy growth and lack of development. Top communist and assorted leftist leaders saw in it a vindication of socialism, apparently not realizing that Chairman Deng had effectively abandoned such notions in 1978 when he charted a new course for China. Many others just denied that this was so and began to dispute the data. However, the prestigious *Economic and Political Weekly* and *The Hindu* published the paper in its entirety, and soon, other newspapers and magazines were quoting from it extensively. It was as if India was till then oblivious to the transformation underway in China!

I then began to realize how inadequate the paper was, as it only skimmed the surface. We needed to do better. Furthermore, since many had challenged the data, we decided to use only data published by prominent international organizations such as the World Bank and IMF, even if it meant that the data would often be somewhat out of date. The World Bank's 2009 studies would, quite understandably, often report 2007 statistics as cross-country tabulations are dependent on when and how the member countries report and are then subject to the World Bank's in-house verification. Thus, quite often, we were using data that seemed out of date, when, in fact, it was the latest.

In 2005, a more substantial paper with the same title was written along with Jeevan Mohanty and Ronald Abraham and this was presented at the China Economic Society's annual conference in Shanghai the following year. It was my first visit to China. This paper was more optimistic about India's long-term prospects and even projected a possibility of India actually over-taking China in the 2040s. A few Chinese economists even challenged this view. But in general, the paper was well received. There were economists from many countries at the Shanghai conference, and soon, I was receiving invitations from many organizations to speak on the subject. The following year, my friend KPR Nair of Pearson Education suggested that I expand this paper into a book. This was when I enlisted Zorawar Daulet Singh, freshly minted out of Johns Hopkins University in the USA with a master's degree in international relations, to work on the project. The first draft was ready in late 2007, and by the time the peer reviews were in, it was mid-2008, and events were moving rapidly. So it was back to the word processors for us. We were done in January 2009. Some numbers required changing. China and India are both battling unprecedented job losses; China more, but India has also been hurting. Both countries face huge contractions of their exports, but our prognosis for the future still holds. India needs to do better if it has to catch up with China.

Mohan Guruswamy

Introduction

1

The emergence of China as a major international actor has been the dominant geopolitical event of the new millennium so far. In the last decade, China has emerged as the largest exporter of manufactured goods to the USA with a favourable merchandise trade balance of approximately US$ 266 billion (total Sino–US trade of US$ 409 billion in 2008) causing it in the recent years to emerge as the biggest holder of US-dollar assets as part of its foreign exchange reserves (US$ 1.95 trillion).[1] Above its treasury holdings, surveys suggest the total dollar share of China's reserves is estimated to range from US$ 1.2 trillion to US$ 1.7 trillion. In 2008, China's financed half—close to US$ 400 billion—of the USA's current account deficit.[2]

In fact, today, the larger Asian economic story is intrinsically linked to the Chinese growth. China now accounts for over 55 per cent of Asian exports, 7.2 per cent of world imports, 16.5 per cent of global import growth, and an astounding 16 per cent of global GDP growth. The US investment bank, Goldman Sachs, estimates that China will account for 36 per cent of the world's incremental GDP between 2000 and 2030.

By early 2007, China had surpassed the United States as the largest exporter to the EU and also displaced the USA as Japan's top trade partner. China's total exports are estimated to reach US$ 1.2 trillion in 2007, surpassing the USA as the world's second-largest exporter just after Germany.[3] Further, observers had anticipated that if China maintained current import- and export-growth rates, it will overtake Germany to become the world's top exporter in 2008, and possibly also surpass Germany to become the world's runner-up in terms of total foreign-trade volume by 2007 or early 2008. China is also the third-largest export market for the United States, and fourth-largest for the EU.

Suffice it to say, Gerald Segal's 1999 *Foreign Affairs* article, 'Does China Matter?' from the vantage point of 2007 appears strange and from a different era:

At best, China is a second-rank middle power... In fact, China is better understood as a theoretical power—a country that has promised to deliver for much of the last 150 years but has consistently disappointed. After 50 years of Mao's revolution and 20 years of reform, it is time to leave the theater and see China for what it is. Only when we finally understand how little China matters will we be able to craft a sensible policy toward it.[4]

To be sure, contemporary discourse also tends to exaggerate China's economic gains. To be a modern industrial power, as one writer notes, 'requires a very high level of autonomous technological capacity, to begin with, as well as sophisticated and innovative industry to make use of it, both of which China today lacks'.[5] For instance, foreign inverted enterprises (which account for a high proportion of Chinese exports) imported goods to the value of 87 per cent of their exports in 2005.[6]

Thus, China's trading statistics may hide more than they reveal about the structure of the Chinese economy, and China's export prowess underscores the high involvement of Western MNCs in China rather than an autonomous, industrial capability. Wang Yiwei, a professor at Fudan University, has perhaps accurately perceived China's current position in the international political economy:

> Presently, the movement of light industry and consumer goods production from advanced industrialized countries to China is nearly complete, but heavy industry is only beginning to move. Developed countries' dependence on China will be far more pronounced following this movement.[7]

While the ascent of China as a global economic actor has inevitably been the dominant theme in international economics literature, the spotlight in recent years has begun to focus upon India as the other big, Asian transformation story. Already, India and China are among the top three economies in the world on the basis of purchasing power parity (PPP). This has inevitably led to a number of comparisons between the two giant neighbours. The trend was set by an article 'Can India Overtake China?', in the US journal *Foreign Policy* in 2003, co-authored by Yasheng Huang and Tarun Khanna. Both come with impressive credentials. Huang is an associate professor at MIT's Sloan School of Management, and Khanna is a professor at the Harvard Business School. In retrospect, it is worth recalling Khanna's conclusions in 2003:

> India is not outperforming China overall, but it is doing better in certain key areas. That success may enable it to catch up with and perhaps even overtake China. Should that prove to be the case, it will not only demonstrate the importance of homegrown entrepreneurship to long-term economic development; it will also show the limits of the FDI-dependent approach China is pursuing.[8]

In the same year, the US investment bank Goldman Sachs released the BRIC acronym in a report that projected the extraordinary economic rise of four emerging economies—Brazil, Russia, India and China— up to the middle of the 21st century.[9]

Subsequently, however, Khanna appears to have revised his earlier perspectives that were clearly more optimistic on India's growth story. His most recent work has assumed a less sanguine if more realistic outlook on India's prospects vis-à-vis her neighbour to the north and he entirely avoids the notion of a race between the two Asian giants.[10]

Nonetheless, the economic historian, Angus Maddison,[11] in an ambitious historical survey has put the contemporary phase in a historical perspective. According to his calculations, from at least the beginning of the Common Era until the early 19th century, China and India accounted for approximately half of global GDP (see Chart 1.1). For much of this period, China and India were intact polities, had the world's largest populations, and were technological leaders.[12] Moreover, while in 2007, both economies accounted for only around 7 per cent of absolute, global output, if current rates of growth are sustained by both, they will resume their historic place in the next few decades. This forecast is underscored by both countries' dedication to economic rejuvenation that is well-recognized.

An international interest in India's economic renaissance has given rise to a self-laudatory mood among India's elite; it is not without some good reason.

Chart 1.1   Major Economies' Share of Global GDP, 0–2005

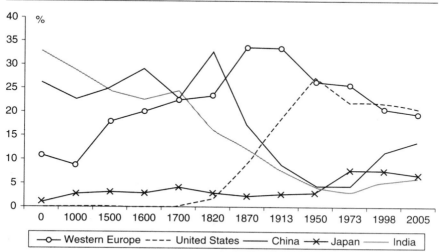

Source: Angus Maddison, *The World Economy: A Millennial Perspective*, OECD Development Centre Studies, 2001; Chart extracted from Saul Eslake, *China and India in the World Economy*, ANZ Bank, July 2005.
Note: A recent World Bank study on improved estimates of different countries' GDP and per capita GDP calculated on a purchasing-power-parity (PPP) basis has revised downwards previous estimates of several economies including India and China. China's revised GDP (PPP) share of global output is 9.7 per cent. India's revised share is 4.3 per cent. A full report can be found at www.worldbank.org/data/icp.

Chart 1.2   Growth Rates, 2004–2008

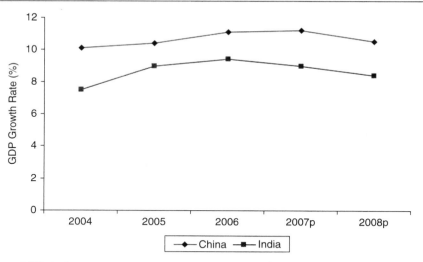

p = IMF Projections
Source: IMF, *The Economist*, OECD

India has been posting a growth of nearly 9 per cent for the last few years (see Chart 1.2). We are simultaneously witnessing spectacular growth rates across the Eurasian geo-economic space. The ASEAN group of nations has been impressing with their economic performance for over a decade, with Vietnam now as the most recent, emerging market success.[13] Even countries such as Bangladesh and Pakistan, the former predicted by Henry Kissinger to become a 'basket case' and the latter considered being well-advanced towards becoming a failed state, have performed well. Importantly, Russia's unprecedented economic–political resurgence over the past few years, a decade after it was all but written-off, has further buttressed the redistribution of economic power toward Eurasia, and has, consequently, re-altered the global balance of economic power.[14] India, however, with its huge labour pool and recent growth rates has the potential to irrevocably tilt the world's economic weight towards Asia.

Many recent studies have indicated how tilted this is likely to become at the midway point of this century. Goldman Sachs has predicted that the world's three largest economies in 2050 will be China, the USA and India (see Chart 1.3). But what is interesting is how far behind the other major economies of the world will be. The next biggest economy, then, will be Japan whose GDP will be about one quarter that of India! This, of course, depends a good deal upon India pressing on with economic and structural reforms.

Chart 1.3   The Largest Economies in 2050

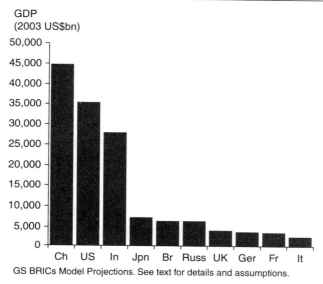

GS BRICs Model Projections. See text for details and assumptions.

Source: http://www2.goldmansachs.com/insight/research/reports/99.pdf

In recent days, the spotlight has also been on the rise of India as well as on the possible impact it may have on India–China relations. Of late, there has been a flurry of interest in both countries as India and China try to re-evaluate where they stand vis-à-vis each other now and in the foreseeable future, the high point being the Wen–Singh joint declaration of a 'Strategic and Cooperative Partnership' in April 2005 in New Delhi. India and China celebrated the 'Year of Friendship' in 2006 and efforts are underway to keep that glow on.

Points of friction have, nonetheless, kept mutual fears and suspicions stoked. The border issue has once again come to the fore on the eve of Chairman Hu Jintao's November 2006 visit, as India was somewhat rudely reminded by the Chinese ambassador to India, Sun Yuxi, that what was generally assumed to be a border problem involving small give-and-takes along the line of actual control (LAC) is, in fact, a territorial dispute with China restating its claim on the north-eastern Indian state of Arunachal Pradesh (formerly the NEFA). Simultaneously, Sino-Indian trade is burgeoning. The Chinese and Indian governments have recently vowed to raise the annual volume of bilateral trade to US$ 60 billion by 2010.[15] While this is happening, both countries are feverishly upgrading and modernizing roads and communications in the border areas. India and China have also embarked on major military modernizations.

Interestingly, Russia and Israel are playing a major role in this area with both countries. India's non-military trade with both countries is negligible, whereas China has a growing energy dependence on Russia. While Russia and China resolved their border dispute in 2005, Russians continue to be wary of a major influx of Chinese nationals into their sparsely inhabited Asian hinterland. But presently, this seems to be in the background, and India, China and Russia have also embarked on the so-called triangular initiative. However, the primary focus of all these three transition economies is toward internal socio-economic rejuvenation manifested by their desire to deepen their integration with global economic processes. This reorientation has ineluctably influenced their foreign policies, where economic realism is compelling them to develop omni-directional relationships in the international system. In such a context, it is hardly surprising that all three actors are also seeking to sustain constructive ties with Washington, albeit on an equal footing.

Thus, however interesting their geopolitical environment may be, for the foreseeable future, both India and China will be preoccupied with their domestic priorities or as a prominent China scholar, David Lampton, has remarked, 'outward-bound but inner-directed'. Both countries have a youthful population with rising aspirations. Both countries are plagued with the consequent problems of growth, with rising inequalities between regions and economic classes. It appears that both countries will be impacted by similar problems.

For the last half a century, since its occupation of Tibet, China has been India's neighbour. Good neighbourliness seemed to have been forgotten soon after as both countries fought a fierce war in 1962. The military defeat has left a searing impression on the Indian psyche. While the process of rapprochement, since it began in the late-1970s, has continued largely uninterrupted, both countries are still wary. India is increasingly aware of the widening economic disparity with China, and China fears that a democratic India may increasingly participate in US designs to 'contain' it. It is not just the Chinese who think this way. The chief of India's dominant Communist Party, Prakash Karat, has publicly stated that his party will not allow China to be encircled. Karat, of course, has made no comment on China's attempts to forge military ties with Bangladesh, Burma and now even Nepal in addition to the well-established patron–client relationship it has with Pakistan. Many in India see this as a Chinese attempt to encircle India!

Indian Foreign Minister, Pranab Mukherjee, recently reiterated India's policy vis-à-vis her northern neighbour. He noted that while New Delhi was 'fully conscious of our outstanding differences with China, including on the boundary question', and that 'some degree of healthy competition' between India and China 'is inevitable' in the economic sphere, 'China remains an important priority of our foreign policy and a key component of our 'Look East' policy'. India remained committed, at the same time, to addressing the differences 'proactively, through peaceful dialogue on an equal footing'. Thus, the 'basic paradigm' of New Delhi's China policy 'is to seek an all-round development of ties, without allowing these differences to define the agenda of the relationship'.[16]

Nonetheless, the current, economic gap is now a matter of great concern in India and there is a wider realization that any political contest for world influence, inevitable to many, will be a no-contest unless the economic gap is substantially closed.[17] While this seems a tall order for India, many pundits are now increasingly confident that India has the potential to meet this formidable challenge.

This book will examine the Sino-Indian economic asymmetry in some depth to give the reader a sense of magnitude of the prevailing gap. The narrative will then proceed to highlight the principal features of the Chinese growth trajectory and the development strategies employed by Beijing's planners since the 'open door' after 1978, which has resulted in, as the World Bank calls it, 'the largest and fastest poverty reduction in history'. It is well-recognized that China's growth pattern—export-driven, manufacturing-led industrialization—has largely emulated the model of her East Asian peers, albeit on a phenomenally larger scale. Since 2000, Chinese international economic interactions have manifested in cross-border trade and investment linkages that have fundamentally re-altered the structure of global product and factor markets. We illustrate this by focusing on the East Asian geo-economic division of labour, where China is now at the epicentre of regional production networks, and which India, for the most part, has excluded itself from.[18] We also, however, show that China's economic rise in Asia is not an autonomous dynamic. Rather, it is one driven by a very high involvement of the USA in the East Asia region with China acting as a manufacturing conduit for economic interactions with the West. Finally, we seek to draw attention to core policy lessons that India could derive as it seeks to reclaim its historical position in the global economic system.

We also believe that there is much that India can learn from the recent Chinese experience and its great success in transforming its economy from a traditional peasant economy to a manufacturing and export powerhouse. Many of the policies adopted by China to encourage the establishment of huge manufacturing capacities by domestic and foreign investors can be considered by India for adoption with some modifications to suit its prevalent political economy. The Chinese experience in transforming its state-owned enterprises (SOEs) from being lethargic, state-owned and bureaucratically controlled ventures into relatively autonomous and vital engines of growth holds many lessons for India grappling with its huge and often inefficient public sector undertakings (PSUs). There are many other lessons to be learnt from China too. Benchmarking to facilitate change is a common management practice and we hope that many of the comparisons we make here will enable India to benchmark itself better.

Despite the spectacular gains of the recent years, both China and India are extremely poor countries. Their per capita incomes now are far below the OECD group of nations, and below even most South American and ASEAN countries. In both countries, the majority of the workforce is dependant on agriculture for sustenance. Yet, there are essential differences. These are highlighted in Chapter 2. India's problems are even more acute, but China's experience shows a way forward. India must industrialize rapidly. India's growth at present is largely sustained by the growth of services. For the period 2002–03 to 2006–07, services contributed 69 per cent of the overall average growth in GDP. It is as if India is becoming a post-industrial economy without having reaped the benefits of industrialization!

According to a recent study, 86 per cent of India's working population, or 395 million workers, constitute the unorganized sector. According to these findings, in 2004–05, 91 per cent of agricultural labourers and 64 per cent of rural and 52 per cent of casual non-agricultural labour force received a wage below the national minimum wage designated by the Central government (Rs 66 per day). Even 57.3 per cent of unorganized, regular workers in rural areas, and 47.2 per cent in urban areas received a wage below this minimum.[19]

In fact, India's poverty-alleviation goal itself remains formidable. The current, official poverty line is in terms of a caloric value, i.e. 2100 calories per day per person in urban areas and 2400 calories in rural areas. The minimum cost of obtaining such nutrition (about 650 grams of grains) was calculated in 1979, when this line was formed. This translates into a poverty line of Rs 454 per month and Rs 327 per month in urban and rural areas respectively. Aside from a three-decade-old nutritional criterion, such a low threshold for poverty does not account for essential, basic, human needs such as healthcare, education, electricity, drinking water, sanitation, clothing, and shelter. After accounting for these fundamental human needs, the poverty line is closer to an income line of Rs 840 per month. At this level, about 69 per cent of India is living in poverty.[20]

Clearly, a growth strategy relying *solely* on skill-based development is simply untenable. Rather, a balanced growth template would ineluctably need to leverage on the massive underemployed labour-surplus in rural India. With approximately 75–110 million young Indians projected to enter the labour force over the next decade, an industrial employment-creating growth strategy assumes vital salience.

However, for this to occur, supply-side constraints—physical infrastructure, energy security, food security, education, healthcare, R&D, S&T—will need to be addressed as part of a coherent strategy for development. As Jagdish Bhagwati noted a decade-and-a-half ago, 'Indian planners underestimated the productive role of better health, nutrition, and education and, hence, underspent on them'.[21] In a similar vein, two noted scholars recently remarked that 'no aspect of India's developmental experience has been so marked by disparities between rhetorical ambitions and actual achievement as our educational system'.[22] This neglect still prevails.

Moreover, reforms in the agricultural sector, which still account for approximately 60 per cent of total employment and the livelihood of 600 million Indians, would need to form an intrinsic part of the template for development. The Chinese experience suggests that it was investment in these vital areas that has underpinned and sustained Chinese growth for over two-and-a-half decades and is likely to do so for the foreseeable future. If India's policy planners are unable to successfully address these core, developmental objectives, India's quest for the great-power status will remain a hollow pipedream.[23]

NOTES

1   As of 31 December 2008, China owns over US$ 700 billion or 18 per cent of foreign-held US treasuries. (Total foreign exchange reserves are as of 2008.) China accounts for 70–80 per cent of total US imports of toys, footwear and other low-end products, nearly 40 per cent of total apparel imports and 35 per cent of consumer electronics.

2   Brad Sester and Arpana Pandey, 'China's $1.7 Trillion Bet', Council on Foreign Relations, January 2009.

3   'China Expected to Overtake US to Become World's Second Largest Exporter', *People's Daily Online*, 21 August 2007.

4   Gerald Segal, 'Does China Matter?', *Foreign Affairs*, September/October 1999.

5   William Pfaff, 'China: The Pretend Superpower', *International Herald Tribune*, 24 August 2007.

6   Source: Shaun Breslin, 'The Political Economy of Development in China: Political Agendas and Economic Realities', Development, 2007, 50(3), pp. 3–10.

7   Wang Yiwei, 'China's Rise: An Unlikely Pillar of US Hegemony', *Harvard International Review*, 22 March 2007.

8   Huang, Yasheng, and Tarun Khanna, 'Can India Overtake China?', *Foreign Policy*, July–August, 2003.

9   See the following report on forward projections on the BRIC economies, Dominic Wilson and Roopa Purushothaman, 'Dreaming with the BRICs: The Path to 2050', Global Economics Paper No. 99, Goldman Sachs, New York, 1 October 2003. (The term BRIC was coined by Jim O'Neill of Goldman Sachs in 2001).

10 Tarun Khanna, *Billions of Entrepreneurs: How China and India Are Reshaping Their Futures—and Yours*, Harvard Business School Press, 2008.

11 Angus Maddison is emeritus professor of economic sociology at the Faculty of Economics, University of Groningen. He enjoys a world-wide reputation as a pioneer in the field of the quantification of economic growth in an international comparative and historical perspective.

12 Angus Maddison, *The World Economy: A Millennial Perspective*, OECD Development Centre Studies, 2001. Also see Angus Maddison, *World Population, GDP and Per Capita GDP, 1-2003 AD*, November 2006; for a critique of Maddison's estimates, see Bryan Haig's review of his *The World Economy: Historical Statistics* (OECD, 2003) in *The Economic Record*, Vol. 81 No. 252 (March 2005), pp. 91–93.

13 Vietnam has been the third-fastest growing economy in Eurasia for the last couple of years.

14 Zorawar Daulet Singh, 'Resurgence of Russia: Commercial Realism Can Benefit India', *The Tribune*, 6 February 2007. (Russia's foreign-currency reserves have surged 35-fold in the last decade to US$ 420 billion, exceeding that of all other countries except China and Japan).

15 Editorial, 'Sino-Indian Ties Cemented', *People's Daily Online*, 15 January 2008.

16 'India Turns Focus on China in "Look East" Policy', *The Hindu*, 15 September 2007; Pranab Mukherjee, P. S. Suryanarayana, 'Strategic Partnership with China Will Mature', *The Hindu*, 18 September 2007.

17 Arun Shourie, 'To Race China, First Let's Get Our Feet off the Brakes', *Indian Express*, 7 November 2006; Ramtanu Maitra, 'Why India's Economy Lags Behind China's', *Asiatimes*, 27 June 2003.

18 Of course, we are referring to the global manufacturing supply-chains. If one views the overall international economic division of labour, three emerging economies stand out—Russia for energy and commodities, China for consumer electronic

goods, India for informational technology-enabled services (ITES)—each having carved a niche supply base.

19 According to *Report on Conditions of Work and Promotion of Livelihood in the Unorganised Sector*, the first authoritative study on the state of informal or unorganized employment in India—compiled by the National Commission for Enterprises in the Unorganized Sector (NCEUS), the Government of India constituted the NCEUSe September 2004 under the Chairmanship of Professor Arjun Sengupta. According to the Commission's definition, 64 per cent of the unorganized-sector workers are in agriculture, while the remaining are in non-agriculture. A majority of these workers—64.8 per cent of agricultural workers and 62.8 per cent of unorganized-sector, non-agricultural workers—are self-employed. Casual wage workers comprise 34.6 per cent of the agricultural workers, and 19.8 per cent of the unorganized-sector, non-agricultural workers. (Access report at: http://nceus.gov.in/ Condition_of_workers_sep_2007.pdf).

20 Mohan Guruswamy and Ronald Joseph Abraham, *Redefining Poverty: A New Poverty Line for a New India*, Centre for Policy Alternatives, New Delhi, February 2006, (Access report at http://cpasindia.org/reports/16-redefining-poverty-line-india.pdf).

21 Jagdish Bhagwati, *India in Transition: Freeing the Economy*, Oxford, UK: Clarendon Press, 1993.

22 Devesh Kapur and Sunil Khilnani, 'Primary Concerns', *Hindustan Times*, 23 April 2006.

23 Zorawar Daulet Singh, 'India's Rising Power: Myth or Reality?', *World Affairs*, Vol. 11, No. 4, Winter 2007.

India Versus China: An Overview of the Major Socio-Economic Indicators

2

ECONOMIC AND SOCIAL COMPARISON

Even with their impressive growth rates in recent years, and despite their emergence in terms of absolute GNP among the world's top ten, both China and India remain excruciatingly poor countries; more so India than China. Table 2.1 below attests to this reality. In 2007, in terms of GNP, China with US$ 3,250 billion ranks third, while India with US$ 1,132 billion ranks tenth. This has given leaders of the two Asian giants' seats on the global high table. Although, when it comes to ranking in terms of per capita income (2005), which is a truer indicator of the condition of the common people, China and India drop off from the first page. India ranks 92nd and China is now just in the 71st place. In recent years, we tend to use purchasing-power-parity (PPP) figures as they show us in a better light, but do not get any better when it comes to ranking, as China and India are ranked 62nd and 82nd respectively.

Even after tinkering with PPP figures, it remains a fact that both countries have stubborn problems with poverty. If we adopt the UNDP's yardstick of US$ 2 a day to provide for basic human needs with a modest modicum of quality in living standards, both China and India still fare poorly. Again, India is more so than China (see Table 2.2 and Table 2.3). But what should trouble the Indian leadership is that the pace of improvement in China seems to offer the prospect of achieving a more egalitarian society in the foreseeable future, while a time frame for a similar situation in India is difficult to pinpoint. Mind you, in a rapidly changing world, relative expectations also rapidly change. This poses yet another challenge (see Table 2.4 and Table 2.5).

With its impressive achievements in the economic sphere, China has, not surprisingly, also fared better in terms of social-sector achievements. The most notable of these is the rapid transformation of China into a highly literate country, and, therefore, better placed for the transition into a modern society. But what should cause Indians concern is that China seems to be doing better

Table 2.1   Top 12 Countries (Nominal GDP) of the World, 2002 and 2007

	2002			2007	
Country	GDP (US$ bn)	Per capita GDP (US$)	Country	GDP (US$ bn)	Per capita GDP (US$)
USA	10,470	36,350	USA	14,020	45,790
Japan	3,919	30,850	Japan	4,382	34,380
Germany	2,025	24,540	**CHINA**	**3,250**	**2,460**
UK	1,582	26,670	Germany	3,235	39,150
France	1,465	24,450	UK	2,731	45,160
CHINA	**1,454**	**1,130**	France	2,540	41,550
Italy	1,224	21,130	Italy	2,110	36,280
Mexico	649	6,330	Brazil	1,267	6,690
S. Korea	547	11,480	Russia	1,183	8,340
INDIA	**508**	**490**	**INDIA**	**1,132**	**1,020**
Brazil	506	2,870	S. Korea	965	19,690
Russia	345	2,380	Mexico	876	8,060

Source: The Economist Intelligence Unit, 2007

Table 2.2   International Poverty Line

	Population below US$ 1 a day	Population below US$ 2 a day
China	16.6	46.7
India	34.7	52.4

Source: World Development Indicators 2006
*The last survey year for China was 2001 and for India it was 1999–2000 so some changes are likely

Table 2.3   National Poverty Line

Country	Survey year	Rural (%)	Urban (%)	National (%)
China	1998	4.6	<2	4.6
India	1999–2000	30.2	24.7	28.6

Source: *World Development Indicators, 2003,* '<' means less than

despite allocating the same percentage of its GNP towards education. This suggests that China seems to be getting more out of its educational system than India. Even though China allocates only one per cent more of its GNP for healthcare, it nevertheless has far more impressive achievements in this sector as well. In recent days, the Indian prime minister has indicated that his number-one priority is to make the government more efficient and responsive to national needs and goals. Clearly, he knows the reality better than most of those holding elected offices and places of authority in the government.

Table 2.4   Human Development Index

Country	1970 HDI Value	Rank	2005 HDI Value	Rank
Sweden	0.881	2	0.956	6
Australia	0.862	12	0.962	3
Canada	0.887	1	0.961	4
Netherlands	0.867	10	0.953	9
USA	0.881	3	0.951	12
Japan	0.875	6	0.953	8
Switzerland	0.872	8	0.955	7
U.K	0.873	7	0.946	16
China	0.372	64	0.777	**81**
India	0.254	82	0.619	**128**

Source: *Statistical Outline of India, 2007–08,* TATA Economic Services

Table 2.5   Social Sector Indicators

Description	India	China
Gross enrolment ratio in primary schools (%)	116.0	118.0
Adult literacy (%)	61	91
Labour cost per worker in manufacturing (US$ per year)	1,192	729
Public education expenditure (% of Govt. expenditure)	10.7	12.8*
Physicians per 1,000 population	0.6	1.5
Health expenditure (% of GDP)	5.0	4.7
Health expenditure per capita (US$)	31.0	71.0
Health expenditure per capita (PPP US$, 2003)	82.0	278.0
Contraceptive prevalence rate (%)	47.0	87.0

Source: Statistical Outline of India, 2007–08, TATA Economic Services
*pertains to 1990

P. Sainath, a leading development scholar in India, has noted that despite deploying more of its GNP for health, India is one of the six most privatized health systems in the world. This is also hopelessly skewed in favour of the urban areas. The health services of the states are woefully understaffed and under provisioned. Rural people, by and large, are forced to fend for themselves when it comes to healthcare. Not surprisingly, Indian rural health spending accounts for the second largest component of rural debt. See Chart 2.1. Among, her BRIC peers, India lags behind on health indicators India's mortality rate (children under five years) is 76 per 1,000, compared to 16 per 1,000 in Russia, 24 per 1,000 in China, and 20 per 1,000 in Brazil.

Chart 2.1 Share of Public Expenditure on Health in Total Health Expenditure, 2000

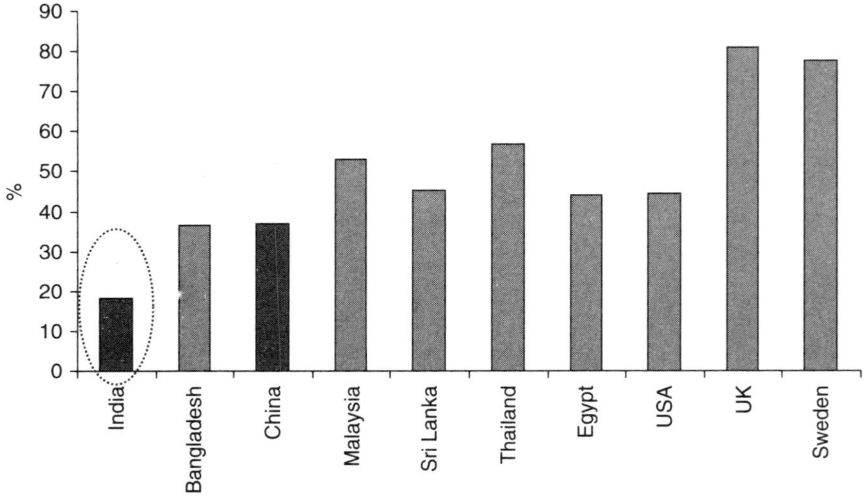

Source: *UNDP Human Development Report, 2003*

The rate of change reflected in the Human Development Index (HDI), which is a composite index prepared by the UNDP using longevity, knowledge and income as its key components, shows the vast superiority of China's achievements in these areas (see Table 2.4). While India's HDI rose from 0.254 in 1970 to 0.611 in 2004, China's rose from 0.372 to 0.768 in the corresponding period. We must not forget that China's per capita income in 1970 was lower than that of India (see graph in Chart 2.2).

In terms of electricity, China's lead over India is truly astounding. It produces more than two and a half times the electricity as India, while the average Chinese consumption is just about that much more. India, however, seems better connected. Even though India is one-third of China in terms of surface area, it has a bigger railway network and road system. This and the greater distances in China, apparently, account for its disproportionately larger air traffic. But it would appear that this gap is closing a bit given the boom that India has been experiencing in air transportation in the last two years (see Table 2.6).

That the Chinese lead in electricity production and consumption is not the entire story. By end 2007, China had an installed generation capacity five times that of India. Furthermore, its far superior power distribution is also telling. The transmission and distribution losses in China are merely 6.8 per cent, while

Chart 2.2   Comparison of Per Capita Income

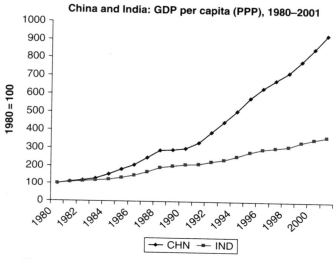

China and India: GDP per capita (PPP), 1980–2001

Source: www.worldbank.org/data/icp

Note: The International Comparison of Prices (ICP) project recently released improved estimates of different countries' GDP and per capita GDP calculated on purchasing power parity (PPP) basis. These new estimates show the Chinese economy to be about 40 per cent smaller in PPP terms than previously thought. The estimate for India too has been revised down by around the same factor. China's revised PPP estimate of per capita GDP in 2005 is US$ 4091; India's is US$ 2126. A full report can be found at www.worldbank.org/data/icp.

Table 2.6   Infrastructure Indicators

Description	India	China
Electricity production (bn kWh)	667.8	2199.6
Electricity consumption Per capita (kWh)	457.0	1,585.0
Rail route (km)	63,465.0	62,200.0
Road network (km)	33,19,644.0	14,02,698.0
Air passengers carried ('000)	27,528.0	136,722.0

Source: *Statistical Outline of India, 2007–08*, TATA Economic Services

India loses 23.4 per cent, much of it to theft. It is little wonder that the average electricity tariff in China is US$ 3.20 per 100 kW lower than that of India. Despite the high tariffs in India, the cumulative loss in 2004 made by the power sector here were Rs 22,013 crore.[1] (Rs 1 crore = Rs 10 million, see Table 2.7).

Not surprisingly, China's lead in other major sectors is also considerable. Its production of food grains is twice as much as India's, giving it a far better per capita availability of food grains. While India's production has risen a good deal, the near static per capita availability of cereals should cause concern, especially since the coming decades are bound to see a rise in

Table 2.7   Energy Profile

Description	India	China
Electricity generating capacity (Mw)	141,500.0	713,000.0
Transmission and distribution losses (% of total power)	23.4	6.8
Electricity tariff (US$/100 kW)	7.53	4.3
Energy use (kg of oil equivalent per capita)	520.0	1,094.0

Source: *World Development Indicators 2006* and *Statistical Outline of India 2004–05*, TATA Economic Services; 'India's Installed Capacity as of End 2007': Ministry of Power, India; 'China's Installed Capacity as of End 2007': Xinhua News Agency, 8 February, 2008

food-grain demand. Many experts suggest that for India to meet its growing demand, food-grain production should rise at nearly 4 per cent as opposed to the current trend of 1.1 per cent[2] (For a detailed analysis of India's agriculture situation, see the CPA study 'The Looming Crisis in Indian Agriculture' available on www.cpasindia.org).

Other indicators that illustrate the vast chasm separating India from China are the production of steel and cement. China now produces ten times steel and six times cement as India. Despite its higher steel production, China has also been in recent years a large importer of Indian iron ore. While coal still accounts for 57 per cent[3] of India's electricity production, its production in India has been languishing. Not least among the causes for this is the fact that the Indian coal industry has largely come under the control of the state and this has been inimical to more efficient mining. China produces four times as much coal as India. On the other hand, India has begun to import coal, despite having huge reserves (see Table 2.8).

Value addition rather than output is always a better indicator of the stage of economic development and industrial growth. A major point of comparison is that China's value addition in industry is almost twice that of India. This, coupled with the fact that China's industrial sector contributes twice as much as that of the Indian industrial sector to their respective GDP,

Table 2.8   Agricultural and Industrial Production

Million tons/year	India	China
Steel production	29	163
Cement production	109	650
Food grain production	210	418
Crude oil production	40	160
Coal production	300	1300

Source: *Statistical Outline of India 2004–05*, TATA Economic Services

clearly suggests that India still has quite some way to go in order to catch up with China in gaining overseas markets and creating employment for the millions joining the work force each year. Two other points of comparison are the greater role that international trade plays in the Chinese economy and its higher gross-capital formation. This suggests that the Chinese lead will continue till the time India embarks on a more determined bid to step up industrial production and capture a bigger share of the international markets (see Table 2.9).

China's external-sector expansion is well recognized. China exports eight times more than India, and its imports are four times India's. China's current account surpluses have accumulated into very large reserves—seven times India's (see Table 2.10).

The lower-tariff structure in China has boosted its exports and has ensured higher investments in the last decade. The simple mean tariff in the case of all products in China in 1992 was 40.4 per cent, which came down to 9.8 per cent in the year 2004. For India also, it has witnessed a decrease, but not as much as in China. Similarly, the simple mean tariff of manufactured products in 2004 in India was 27.9 per cent, whereas China's tariff was one-third of that in India, with 9.7 per cent in the same year (see Table 2.11).

Table 2.9   Economic Highlights, 2003

Per cent of GDP	India	China
Agro value added	22	15
Industry value added	27	52
Exports of goods and services	14	34
Imports of goods and services	16	32
Gross capital formation	24	44

Source: *World Development Indicators, 2005*

Table 2.10   External Sector Comparison, End-2008

US$ Billion	India	China
Exports	176	1465
Imports	287	1156
Current account	−38	416
Foreign reserves	250	1951

Source: *CIA World Factbook,* World Bank

Table 2.11   Tariff Barriers in India and China

Country	All products (simple mean tariffs %)		Manufactured products (simple mean tariffs %)	
	1992	2004	1992	2004
India	79.0	28.3	79.9	27.9
China	40.4	9.8	40.6	9.7

Source: *World Development Indicators, 2006*

POST-REFORMS PERFORMANCE

A comparison of the first ten years in the performances of India and China after reforms (from 1992 for India and from 1979 for China) is instructive. China entered the first decade of reforms as a fast-developing and modernizing country with an average decadal growth rate of 5.52 per cent, but more importantly than this, was the performance of its reduction of infant mortality to 42 per 1000 by 1980, elevating life expectancy to 67 years, and raising adult literacy to 66 per cent. India by contrast, had a better growth rate of 5.7 per cent in the 1980s, but came burdened with an infant mortality of 119 per 1000, life expectancy of 59.2 years, and adult literacy of 48.41 per cent (see Table 2.12). According to the recent national-family-health survey 3 (NFHS-3) for 2005–06, 'healthy life expectancy at birth' (HALE), which adjusts the normal life-expectancy measure for years of serious illness/injury predicted from the data, for a girl baby in India in 2002 was only 54 years compared to 65 in China, 68 in Mexico, and 71 in the USA. Further, 46 per cent of young children in India are underweight for their age, compared to 6 per cent in China, 20 per cent in Indonesia, 31 per cent in Pakistan, and 27 per cent in Nigeria. Bihar and Uttar Pradesh were the worst-scoring states on health parameters, while Tamil Nadu and Kerala were the best performing.[4]

Many reasons have been advanced for China's extraordinary performance. Few are as valid as what Amartya Sen wrote: 'China's relative advantage over

Table 2.12   Social Indicators at Pre-reform Stage

	China in 1980	India in 1991
IMR (per 1000)	42	119
Life expectancy (years)	67	59.2
Adult literacy (%)	66	48.41

Sources: India Health Report, UNESCO; *World Development Indicators, 2003*; Sen and Dreze[5]

India is a product of its pre reform (pre 1979) groundwork rather than its post reform redirection.'

Yet another comparison would be even more instructive. In 1978, at the inception of its reforms, China's per capita GDP (in constant 1995 US$) was US$ 148, whereas that of India in the same year, was US$ 236. Seven years after it began its reforms in 1986, China caught up with India in per capita GDP terms (US$ 278 versus US$ 273) and a decade after reforms, in 1988, was comfortably ahead of India with a per capita GDP of US$ 342 compared with India's US$ 312 (see Chart 2.2). In the first post-reform decade, the Chinese economy grew at 10.1 per cent, while the Indian economy grew at 5.7 per cent in the corresponding decade (see Chart 2.3 and Table 2.13). Quite clearly, that was India's lost decade.

But what did India achieve in the first decade of its reforms? In 1992, the first year of its reforms, India's per capita GDP was US$ 331. This grew to US$ 477 in 2001. During the same period, the Chinese per capita GDP surged from US$ 426 to US$ 878 in 2001. In the 1990s, China grew at the

Chart 2.3   Growth Rate Comparison of First Ten Years of Reform

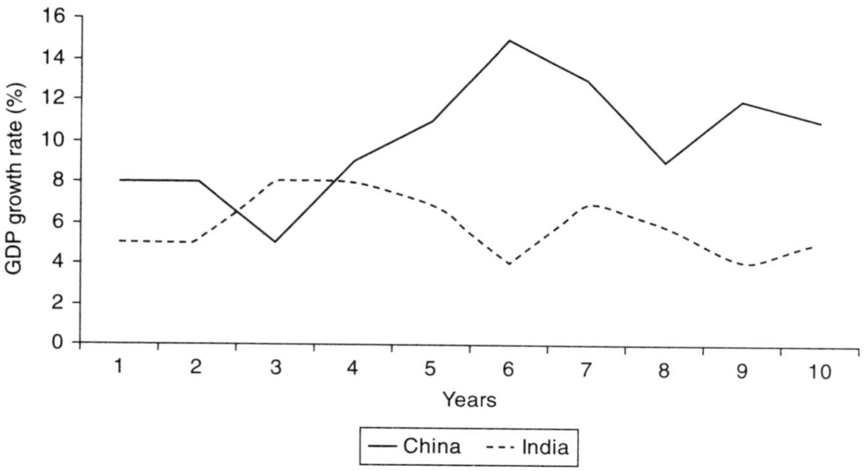

Table 2.13   Growth Rates (Per Cent)

	China	India
Pre reform period	5.52	5.7
Post reform period (First 10 years)	10.1	5.9

Source: Calculated from *World Development Indicators*

Table 2.14   GDP and Population

	1978	2007	Annual growth rate(2000–04)
China			
Population (m)	962.6	1,323.1	1.35
GDP (US$ bn)	141.06	3,250.2	9.4
India			
Population (m)	648	1,110.4	2.51
GDP (US$ bn)	155	1,131.9	6.2

Sources: *World Development Indicators, 2006*; National Accounts Statistics (India) and *China Statistical Yearbook*; The Economist Intelligence Unit

rate of 9.7 per cent, while India grew at 5.9 per cent. Quite clearly, from the beginning, India failed to catch up; instead, it fell well behind China.

China's GDP (1995 constant US$) had grown eightfold since 1979 and stood at US$ 1.4 trillion in 2003; in 1978, Chinese GDP was lower than that of India in absolute terms, but caught up with India in the very next year. In 2007, the size of the Chinese economy (projected at US$ 3.2 trillion) was almost three times that of India. India's GDP stood at US$ 1.1 trillion with a population of 1.09 billion. We seem to be catching up with China on the population front but China's GDP still remains a distant target (see Table 2.14).

A STUDY IN CONTRASTS

It is true that both the countries have transformed themselves after they embarked on the path of economic reforms, but the transformations were entirely different. In 1980, the sectoral break up of China's economy was as follows: agriculture 30 per cent, industry 49 per cent, and services 21 per cent. In 1990, that changed to agriculture 27 per cent, industry 42 per cent, and services 31 per cent. In 2003, that picture transformed further. Agriculture fell to 15 per cent, industry grew further to 53 per cent, while services steadied at 32 per cent. Note the growth in the share of industry now (see Table 2.15). The Indian sectoral picture makes for a study in contrasts. The share of agriculture fell somewhat from 31 per cent in 1990 to 23 per cent in 2003. The share of industry, too, fell from 28 per cent to 26 per cent. Services grew from 41 per cent to 52 per cent (see Table 2.15). Software apart, the biggest contributing factor to the growth of India's services sector has been the growth of public administration. The total consumption expenditure of the government (including defence and other

Table 2.15   Sectoral Break-up of GDP (Per Cent)

	1980	1990	2003	2006
Agriculture				
China	30.1	27.1	15	11.8
India	42.8	31	23	18.5
Industry				
China	48.5	41.6	53	48.7
India	21.9	28	26	26.4
Services				
China	21.4	31.3	32	39.5
India	35.3	41	52	55.1

Sources: *China Statistical Yearbook, 2001; Statistical Outline of India, 2004–05*, TATA Economic Services; and *World Development Indicators, 2006*; 2006 figures – India data from RBI Annual Report 2007, China data from *China Economic Quarterly, 2007 Q2*

government administration) bounded along at 11.73 per cent[6] annually from Rs 26,864.6 crore in 1992–93 to Rs 127, 078.3 crore in 2006–07.[7] The total expenditure on wages and salaries, combined with the pensions for the Central and state governments stood at Rs 198, 260 crore in 2006–07.[8] This kind of spending was not what Keynes had in mind when he advocated public spending to stimulate the economy!

The impact of these sectoral growth rates is reflected in the job creation patterns for the two nations (see Table 2.16). Today China's workforce is 705 million (1999). About half of this workforce or 353 million is employed in agriculture, 28 per cent or 190 million in services, and 22 per cent or 162 million in industry. By contrast India's total workforce is 397 million (1999). The major employer is still the agricultural sector with 60.5 per cent or 240 million, industry is a relatively small 16.8 per cent or 67 million, services seems to be rising but employs merely 22.7 per cent or 90 million (of this, government alone accounts for 19.42 million). Quite clearly, in terms of employment, India is more an agrarian society (see Table 2.17).

Table 2.16   Sectoral Growth Rates, 1980–2004

	1980s		1990s		2000–05	
	China	India	China	India	China	India
Agriculture	5.9	3.1	4	3	3.9	2.5
Industry	11.1	6.9	13.1	6.1	10.9	7.5
Services	13.5	6.9	8.9	7.9	10.0	8.5

Source: *World Development Indicators, 2006* and *Statistical Outline of India 2007–08*, TATA Economic Services

Table 2.17   Sector-wise Employment (Per Cent)

	China	India
Agriculture	43	60.5
Industry	25	16.8
Services	32	22.7

Sources: *China Statistical Yearbook,* various issues, CIA – *The World Factbook* – https://www.cia.gov/library/publications/the-world-factbook/fields/2048.html (accessed on 29 January 2008)

VALUE ADDITION IN MANUFACTURING

The value addition in manufacturing indicates the degree of industrial activity in the country. Clearly, China adds much more value in manufacturing than India. In 2001, China had US$ 407 billion value addition in manufacturing, whereas India added just one-sixth of that with only US$ 67 billion. The gross-output share of the manufacturing sector, in GDP, of China was 39 per cent, which was more than double of that of India (16 per cent) in the year 2003. The output of the services sector as a percentage of GDP stood better for India with 51 per cent in 2003, whereas China's gross output in the services sector remained 33 per cent in the same year (see Table 2.18).

WHO IS INVESTING IN CHINA?

This was primarily made possible by overseas foreign direct investment (FDI), which amounted to US$ 290 billion (Ministry of Foreign Trade and Economic Cooperation, Beijing) during the decade (see Table 2.19).

Apart from the millions of jobs created, the role of FDI in making China a major manufacturing centre in the world is seen in the share of FDI enterprises in total exports, which rose from under 2 per cent to 45.5 per cent in 1999. In India, it was just 8 per cent. The shares of world trade in the GDPs of the two countries, not surprisingly, are also very different. While trade accounts for almost three-fourths (75 per cent) of China's GDP, it accounts for over a third (37 per cent) of India's in 2008. Also, while

Table 2.18   Value Addition and Output

	Value added in manufacturing (US$ bn.)		Manufacturing value added (% of GDP)		Service value added (% of GDP)	
	1990	2001	1990	2003	1990	2003
China	117	407.5	33	39	31	33
India	21	67.1	17	16	41	51

Source: *World Development Indicators, 2005*

Table 2.19   FDI Statistics for China and India

Year	China Foreign direct investment, net inflows, BOP, current US$ million	Gross foreign direct investment (% of GDP)	India Foreign direct investment, net inflows, BOP, current US$ million	Gross foreign direct investment (% of GDP)
1990	3487	1.22	162	0.00
1991	4366	1.40	74	0.03
1992	11,156	3.62	277	0.11
1993	27,515	7.39	550	0.20
1994	33,787	6.60	973	0.33
1995	35,848	5.41	2143	0.64
1996	40,179	5.18	2425	0.69
1997	44,237	5.48	3576	0.90
1998	43,750	5.30	2635	0.65
1999	38,753	5.54	2168	0.50
2000	38,399	4.32	2315	0.58
2001	46,900	4.1	3400	0.71
2002	52,700	4.2	3400	0.68
2003	53,500	3.8	4300	0.72
2004	60,600	—	5,500	—
2005	72,400	2.8	6,600	0.68

Source: *World Development Indicators, 2002; Statistical Outline of India, 2006–07,* TATA Economic Services

China enjoys a 6 per cent share of total world trade, India's share in world trade is 1.5 per cent (see Table 2.20).

In recent days, there has been much speculation as to whether the FDI gap between China and India is indeed as large as it is made out to be. One problem is that the Chinese FDI data is overstated.[9] Since the early 1990s, researchers with the International Monetary Fund (IMF), World Bank and other international institutions have developed an evolving view that about a quarter or more of China's officially recorded FDI is in fact not FDI at all.

Table 2.20   International Linkages

	Total Foreign debt* (US$ bn)	Foreign debt GDP (%)	Foreign debt Foreign reserves (%)	Percentage share of world trade (2006)	Foreign reserves (US$ bn.) (2008)
China	375.0	12.0	19.0	6.0	1,951.0
India	230.0	20.0	92.0	1.5	250.0

Source: *Statistical Outline of India, 2006–07,* TATA Economic Services; Centre for Policy Alternatives Research, WTO statistics; Reserve Bank of India; China's State Administration of Foreign Exchange (SAFE).

*As of end December 2008.

Instead, it is mainland Chinese monies that have flowed out to access better financial, regulatory and legal services and 'round-trip' by returning to China, as apparent FDI to access the fiscal incentives and improved investor protection offered in China to foreign investors.[10] If this argument by IMF and World Bank holds true, then the total FDI inflows into China in 2003 contracts to around US$ 35 billion instead of US$ 53.8 billion, which is what the Chinese official figures show. Chinese (and IMF) FDI figures include what are classified in India as Foreign Institutional Investor (FII) investments in equity markets, loans, etc., while in India, FDI implies only direct investment in industries.[11] Even if these adjustments are made, FDI in China dwarfs India's share. To be sure, recently, India was attracting high FDI inflows that reached US$ 16.4 billion in 2006–07. It was expected to be nearly US$ 30 billion in 2008–09. The composition of recent inflows in India suggests that private equity and portfolio capital rather than MNC-related FDI has dominated FDI inflows. This has implications, as while private equity contributes primarily to management and is relatively focused on short-time horizons, MNC-related FDI brings permanent technology and export linkages with the parent firm along with management innovations.[12] China's FDI base has largely relied on the latter mode.[13]

ADMINISTRATIVE DECENTRALIZATION AND EXPENDITURE

On the face of it, China seems to be deploying just about the same proportion of its GNP towards education and health, yet seems to be achieving better results. Quite clearly, there are lessons to be learnt. While under the communist system, supreme power may be centralized with a small non-elected leadership, it is equally true that the management of the economy and services, like education and healthcare, are greatly decentralized. By contrast, India with a supposedly different political system has become highly centralized and nothing reflects this better than the pattern of expenditure on salaries for government employees (see Chart 2.4 and Chart 2.5). The percentage share of Central government salaries and expenses of the total under this head in China has been continuously declining and has come down from a high of 73.9 per cent in 1953 to 28.9 per cent in 1998. The corresponding trend in India is quite discouraging as it continues to hover around at 40 per cent (see Table 2.21). Quite evidently, the Chinese government is moving downwards to the tiers that have a greater interaction with the people, whereas in India, decentralization is as distant a goal now, as it was in the early years of the Republic.

Chart 2.4   Decentralization in China

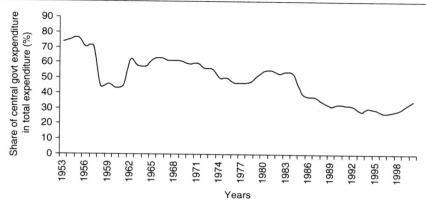

Source: *China Statistical Yearbook,* various issues

Chart 2.5   Centralization in India

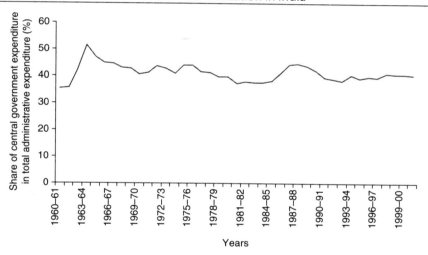

Source: *National Accounts Statistics,* various issues

Table 2.21   Central Government Expenditure
as Per Cent of Total Expenditure

	China	India
1962	61.6	42.23
1970	58.9	41.1
1980	54.3	37.25
1990	32.6	39.42
2000	34.7	40.41

Source: *China Statistical Yearbook,* various issues

However, there is another perspective to the Indian case that is not captured in Chart 2.5. The central liberalization and structural adjustment embodied in the 1991 reforms did lead to a deregulation of the Indian economy. Yet, this process was followed by regional re-regulation as sub-national elites evolved their own agendas in the face of central-policy changes to respond to region-specific policy dilemmas. Thus, 'it is plausible to argue that liberalization in India amounted not to deregulation but to the reordering of state–market relations mediated by sub-national re-regulation strategies and processes'.[14]

This assessment is expressed in the following comments by a corporate executive in India in 1995:

> Most of us who have been dealing with the corridors of power in Delhi for the past 10 years probably now feel that the visits to Udyog Bhavan (Ministry of Industry, Central government) have declined dramatically, may have even disappeared… But, unfortunately the visits and the interaction required with the state governments and the district authorities has in fact gone up dramatically. Why is deregulation at the Centre leading to increased regulation at the state (level)?[15]

And such 'different political responses by political and social groups continue to persist driving the regionally diverse pattern of investment flows and corresponding growth patterns'.[16] According to Aseema Sinha, an approach, 'that focuses only on macro-state institutions, is deeply flawed'. On the other hand, Sinha's 'micro-institutional analysis' suggests, that 'after 1996, with the onset of regionalized coalition governments, central–regional conflict has been displaced to the national cabinet'. Moreover, 'if legislatures fail to act as arenas for the expression and accommodation of local and regionally based interests—as in India—intergovernmental bargaining and negotiation within the central state may become more important'.[17] In sum, India's contemporary political economy, where 'diverse regional elites' interests may hold a veto over central affairs, suggests that a 'bottom-up' approach to reforms analysis may yield additional insights. This is further underscored by the divergence in regional economic performance in the post-reform period.

COMPARATIVE R&D AND EDUCATION CAPABILITIES

At a timely speech in October 2006, Prime Minister Manmohan Singh announced plans to increase research and development (R&D) expenditure from the current share of 0.8 per cent to 2 per cent of GDP in the next five years. The R&D expenditure for India, in absolute terms, is up threefold over the last decade. While 80 per cent of R&D in India is still government-funded, and 60 per cent of this goes towards defence, the so called 'strategic enclaves' of the military–industrial complex—with very few commercial spin offs—this picture is changing, as private investment in R&D is now rising faster than government spending.

Government expenditure on science rose by 24 per cent in 2005 to reach US$ 4.5 billion, suggesting that a shortage of funds is no longer a constraint for Indian innovation. Rather, it is the lack of institutional relationships—both within the educational system (i.e., separation of teaching and research) and between the government and the private sector, that poses the biggest challenge to India's R&D capabilities. A 2005 World Bank study notes, 'India is still a relatively closed economy compared with other Asian economies. India should increasingly tap into the rapidly growing stock of global knowledge through channels such as foreign direct investment, technology licensing, and so on, so that it can catch up with countries like China, where reforms have moved ahead much more rapidly.'[18]

On the World Bank's latest knowledge-economy index, which takes into account not just R&D, but the entire ecosystem that allows R&D efforts to translate into macroeconomic success, India scored 2.8 in 1995 and a marginally lower 2.71 in the most recent score card. China, by way of comparison, has raised its score from 2.83 in 1995 to 4.26 in the most recent score card, and Brazil from 4.73 to 5.1, while Russia has remained more or less at the same score of 5.9.

China's spending on R&D has risen at an annual rate of 18 per cent since 1995, reaching US$ 41 billion by 2006 (see Table 2.22 and Chart 2.7). According to NBS statistics, the bulk of this spending came from private enterprises (71 per cent), followed by the government (19 per cent), and university spending (9 per cent). In December 2006, the Organization for Economic Cooperation and Development (OECD) after evaluating China's R&D spending **on a PPP basis**, announced that China had moved ahead of Japan for the first time, to become the world's second-highest R&D investor

Table 2.22   China's R&D Spending Targets

Year	R&D Spending (all sources, US$ billions)	% of GDP	Central Government (US$ billions)
2004	24.6	1.23	8.7
2010	45.0	2.00	18.0
2020	113.0	2.50	*Not known*

Source: James Wilsdon and James Keeley, 'China: The Next Science Superpower?' in Charles Leadbeater and James Wilsdon, *The Atlas of Ideas: Mapping the New Geography of Science*, DEMOS, January 2007)

after the USA.[19] As per the OECD, the country is expected to invest US$ 136 billion in research and development this year after growing by more than 20 per cent in the past year, ahead of the US$ 130 billion from Japan, but still well behind the US$ 330 billion that the USA will invest. A recent decision by the government is to build up industry-research alliances in the four 'backbone' sectors: steel, coal, chemicals, and agricultural equipment, aimed at upgrading industries that tend to lag. Foreign competitors will receive priority in financing and other support from the Ministry of Science and Technology.[20] In aggregate, this is likely to further buttress productivity and indigenous innovation in China (see Chart 2.6).

China scores over India on major parameters such as the number of researchers in R&D (India has 119 per million population versus 708 for China, according to the World Bank's knowledge-assessment methodology (or KAM), the number of scientific articles, patents or even the proportion of high-tech exports as a proportion of total manufacturing exports (30 per cent versus India's 5 per cent). See Chart 2.8 and Chart 2.9 to have an idea about the doctoral degrees attained by the two economies since 1985.

On the other hand, according to the World Bank's KAM, private firms in India are more geared towards R&D. On a score of 1 to 7, Indian firms score 4.2 versus China's 3.6 when it comes to spending and 5.8 versus 5.1 in terms of technology absorption.

Chart 2.6   China Experiencing 'Reverse-Drain' Largely from the USA

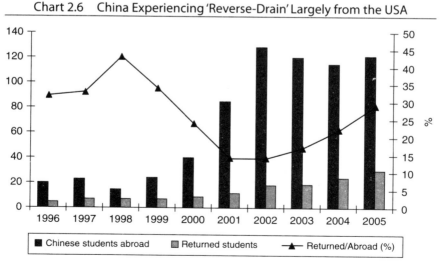

Source: OECD Reviews of Innovation Policy: China, 2007

Chart 2.7   Percentage of Worldwide R&D Spending

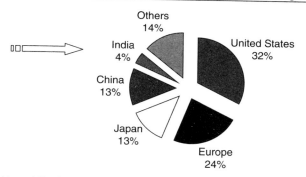

Source: Battelle Memorial Institute and R&D Magazine's 2007 Global R&D Report; Technology report from Europe: 'R&D Paradigm Shifting', by Drew Wilson, contributing writer—*Electronic Business*, 20 March 2007, www.edn.com

Chart 2.8   Number of Science and Engineering (S&E) Doctoral Degrees

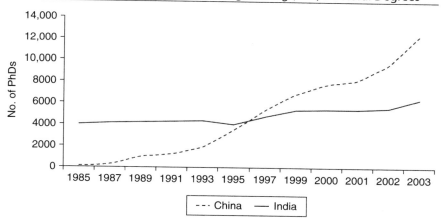

Source: 2008 Science and Engineering Indicators, National Science Board, National Science Foundation, Arlington, VA, USA; http://www.nsf.gov/statistics/seind08/

India produces around 6,000 science and engineering Ph.D.s each year according to Demos, a UK based think tank, as compared to China's 15,000. But more importantly, China has stepped up the internationalization of its research system, with extensive collaborative networks across Europe, Japan and the USA. By the end of 2007, according to the PRC Ministry of Commerce, multinational corporations had established 1,160 R&D centres in China. The Indian system, in contrast, remains relatively insulated mired in structural

Chart 2.9   Number of Science Doctoral Degrees

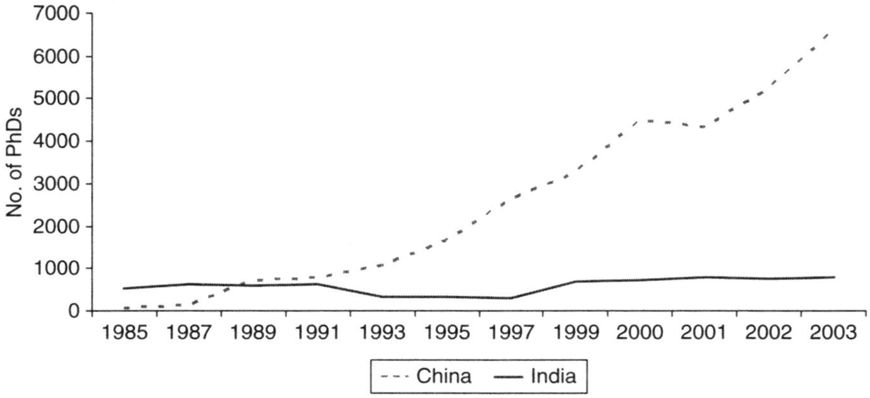

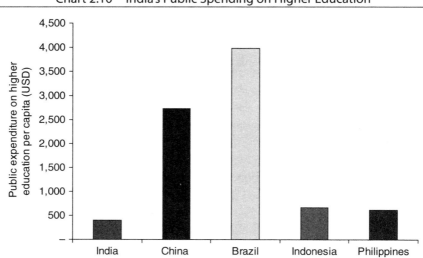

Source: 2008 Science and Engineering Indicators, National Science Board, National Science Foundation, Arlington, VA, USA; http://www.nsf.gov/statistics/seind08/

problems.[21] The Asian Development Bank recently noted that education in India was lagging behind rapid economic growth, with only 12,000 training and vocational institutes, compared to half a million in China. Even in her so called peer group, BRIC, India has the most work to do in expanding education[22]. According to United Nations Educational Scientific and Cultural

Chart 2.10   India's Public Spending on Higher Education

Source: Konark Sharma, 'FDI in Higher Education: Aspirations and Reality', (Mainstream, Vol XLV No 25, 9 June 2007)

Organisation (UNESCO), India's per student public expenditure of US$ 400 is the lowest among developing countries (see Chart 2.10).

In fact, the overall educational system, which presumably serves as the lifeline for an innovative society, is itself in a state of decay in India. This was recently summed up by two prominent scholars; 'in what is otherwise a dismal scene—dilapidated school houses, dysfunctional universities, declining morale—the few oases of success have attracted disproportionate attention'. Further, a distorted policy bias perpetuates the current imbalance in tertiary education. The 'oases of success' as embodied by the Indian Institutes of Technology (IITs) and Indian Institutes of Management (IIMs), together account for merely 1,000 seats per year.[23] According to the charts provided by the Department of Secondary and Higher Education, the budgeted expenditures for IITs is Rs 648 crore, for the IIMs is Rs 64 crore and the overall budget for the University Grants Commission (UGC) is Rs 1,927 crore, which is surprising, since the latter supports more than hundred times the number of students that enter the IITs and yet, proportionally, it receives less than three times the funds.[24] Moreover, the absence of capacity creation in the IITs and IIMs has exacerbated access to even the 'oasis' institutions. The ineluctable outcome is that only around 8 per cent to 11 per cent of young adults have access to higher education compared to Philippines (31 per cent), Thailand (19 per cent), Malaysia (27 per cent) and China (13 per cent).

Yet, this is only half the story. Despite its abysmally low penetration, India still has the world's third-largest system of higher education (after China and the USA), with 10.5 million students enrolled at 17,973 institutions (348 universities and 17,625 colleges), according to 2005–06 figures. In 2005, these institutions turned out nearly 700,000 graduates in the science and engineering disciplines alone. However, several recent surveys by the private sector in India have suggested that only 10 per cent–25 per cent of Indian graduates are employable in modern industry and in MNCs, in particular.[25] For the private sector, this has usually led to in-house retraining programmes that seek to buttress the quality of newly recruited graduates. Mediocrity has inevitably seeped into the teaching profession itself. Only about one-third of the nation's 472,000 academics hold Ph.D.s.[26]

Such a massive supply–demand quantity and quality deficit has led to the emergence of privately funded education, primarily in the realm of professional education—engineering, medicine, and business. Indeed, almost 90 per cent of new capacity over the past decade has been financed by the private sector. Of this, only 30 per cent is supplemented by government financial support. The remainder is composed of 'unaided' private institutions.

Yet, almost all are stifled by the 'license raj' type regulations, with only a select few institutions—that have managed to achieve an autonomous legal status—striking academic excellence. Thus, despite non-state participation, 'virtually no pedagogical innovation or excellence is associated with private institutions, because they are all determined by roughly the same curricular guidelines and rubrics as public institutions'.[27] Furthermore, the fact that 80 per cent of Indian students are not enrolled in technical higher education, which has drawn the largest contribution of private investment, implies that de facto privatization has bypassed the majority of students.

Another major side-effect of supply deficit for quality higher education has been the massive flight of intellectual capital from India. India's 'education imports' approximate to US$ 4 billion per year on higher-education services.

Mehta and Kapur (2004) have perhaps summed it up:

> Over the course of the 1970s and 1980s, politicians acquired a great vested interest in the affairs of universities, seeing them as possible sites for not just political recruitment, but expanding patronage. The direct interference of the state has implied that in most states, universities have become appendages of government offices.

Thus, 'Indian higher education is in a regulatory environment where the private sector will not be deregulated, FDI will not be permitted (even "closed" China permits more FDI in education), the state sector is strapped for resources because of the government's fiscal constraints, and public education cannot mobilize higher funds because of ideological commitments.[28]

A 2005 World Bank study notes that, 'to create a sustained cadre of "knowledge workers", India needs to make its education system more demand driven to meet the emerging needs of the economy and to keep its highly qualified people in the country. This means raising the quality of all higher-education institutions, not just a few world-class ones, such as the Indian Institutes of Technology.'[29] Thus, India's economic managers need to adopt a holistic approach to R&D, with an increasing emphasis on the fundamental role of the country's higher educational system.

This implies a two-pronged approach. First, capacity creation, which given the fiscal constraints, suggests that the private sector will need to share the major economic cost of subsequent expansion. Currently, 'the education system remains suspended between over regulation by the state on the one hand, and a discretionary privatization that is unable to mobilize private capital in productive ways'.[30] Second, creating an intellectual infrastructure for innovation closely aligned to business and social needs, rather than a narrow focus on R&D expenditure and that too in insulated 'enclaves'. Third, the prevailing structure also has implications for regulatory reform. While, under the Indian Constitution, education is primarily the responsibility of India's 31 states, the central government exercises significant regulatory power. Now, with the growing primacy of the private sector as the dominant provider of higher education, such a structure is simply unsustainable. Suffice it to say, the state will need to reorient its role toward a facilitator—integrating and coordinating civilian and military research, regulating higher education, but by acknowledging the reality of private education[31], and expanding capacity in the few high-quality, centrally funded institutions (IITs/IIMs) that continue to flourish.

Obviously, none of this can be successfully implemented without a complete overhaul of the prevailing institutional arrangements.

ENERGY SECURITY

Recently, we have seen crude-oil prices explode to over $120 per barrel level. The International Energy Agency (IEA) in a recent report predicted that global oil demand will rise faster than expected up to 2012 while production lags behind, suggesting that market conditions for energy importers will remain adverse for the next decade.[32] Apart from geopolitical risks, lack of new upstream fields coming online and stagnation in downstream refining capacities, it is the rising emerging market demand that is contributing to the price rise. According to the IEA statistics, China, Russia, India, and the Middle East in 2008 will consume more oil collectively (20.67 m b/d) than the USA for the first time.[33]

In both the countries, oil sectors are largely controlled by National Oil Companies (NOCs). China has demonstrated that they can move with far greater alacrity when it comes to securing international sources of production. The Chinese oil industry has outbid Indian attempts to buy into international oilfields for an assured share of the output. Quite clearly, in the years to come, India and China will begin to compete more vigorously for access to international oil and gas reserves. So far, China seems better placed. But there is more nuance to China's global acquisition spree. In 2006, China's NOCs pumped a combined total of 685,000 barrels per day of oil abroad—less than one per cent of world oil production—and sold at least two-thirds of it in the international market. Thus, contrary to popular belief, China is not locking up oil reserves solely for captive use. Rather, China's NOCs are actually expanding, rather than contracting, the amount of oil available to other consumers by pumping oil abroad, especially at oil fields in which Western companies are either unable or unwilling to invest.[34]

This notion is perhaps more valid for the oil rather than the gas sector, which lacks the fungibility of oil and is characterized by a more fragmented industry structure and, hence, more susceptible to geopolitical variables.

The tight interdependence between a buyer and a seller via gas pipelines is well recognized. The alternative transport option is via shipped liquefied natural gas (LNG). However, achieving economically competitive LNG trade entails building large-scale facilities that require US$ 5–7 billion of capital investment for exploration, development, liquefaction, shipping, and re-gasification. In order to raise such large amounts of capital, to get the gas to the market, the LNG industry has typically relied on long-term (20-year) contracts between the gas supplier and the gas buyer as a way to reduce market risk for lenders. This is a significant difference, as compared to the oil industry where producers develop resources without contracted buyers and then sell the product into the high-volume and heavily traded global oil market. In the case of LNG, neither consumer nor supplier can rely on buying or selling significant volumes without securing a long-term contract, as only about 8 per cent of global LNG is traded under short-term and spot market terms. Thus, LNG, too, is not entirely flexible (creates energy interdependence between seller and buyer).

NATURAL GAS VITAL FOR BOTH COUNTRIES

Natural gas is relatively amongst the most efficient and environmentally friendly of all fossil fuels. Further, it has multiple applications as an efficient feedstock—power, petrochemicals, and fertilizers. However, in China and India, natural gas is currently a minor source in the overall energy mix, representing only three per cent and eight per cent, respectively, of the total primary energy consumption in 2004. Of late, both countries are rapidly expanding infrastructure to serve the demand. China received its first ever LNG cargo in mid-2006 under a long-term contract signed with Australia in 2002. This was buttressed by PetroChina's recent LNG import deals worth US$ 45 billion with Australia.[35] Russia too is likely to gradually emerge as a major energy supplier for China.[36] India also needs to urgently revaluate the transport options of Iranian gas. India signed a five-million-tonne-per-year LNG sale–purchase agreement (SPA) for US$ 22 billion with Iran in June 2005 for 25 years (2009 onward). The geopolitical flux along India's western land frontiers and beyond implies that LNG imports from Iran and Qatar offer a feasible 'second best' solution. Myanmar, too, is likely to become an important source for natural gas imports.[37] Of course, any external transport option would require a domestic gas grid to re-transport gas to the major demand centres. It is estimated that 10,000 km of the 17,000 km new pipelines across India will cater to gas transport.

EXPECTED RISE OF POWER SECTOR'S SHARE IN 2010

According to the Indian Petroleum Ministry projections, natural gas's share of primary energy consumption would rise from the current 8 per cent to 20 per cent by 2025. The largest demand is projected to come from the power sector (71 per cent of incremental demand). The current deficit has resulted in the shutdown of several gas-fired power plants and fertilizer plants (see Chart 2.11).

Unless new sources are tapped, supply-deficit is projected to widen (see Chart 2.12).

Another crucial point on the energy issue and one that the current discourse rarely highlights is that for all the hype in China's hydrocarbon acquisitions globally, it is still relatively self-sufficient in terms of its overall energy supply. China's energy strategy has focused on expanding domestic supply and it has

Chart 2.11   Gas Emerging as a Vital Fuel in India's Energy-Mix

CURRENT GAS SCENARIO
(*Daily average in mmscmd**)

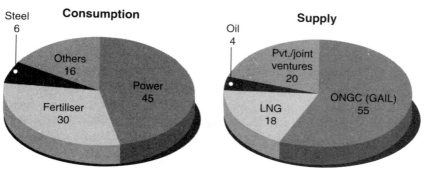

Total 97 mmscmd

*mmscmd million metric standard cubic metres per day

Source: *Business India*, 26 March 2006

Chart 2.12   Natural Gas: Projected Demand–Supply

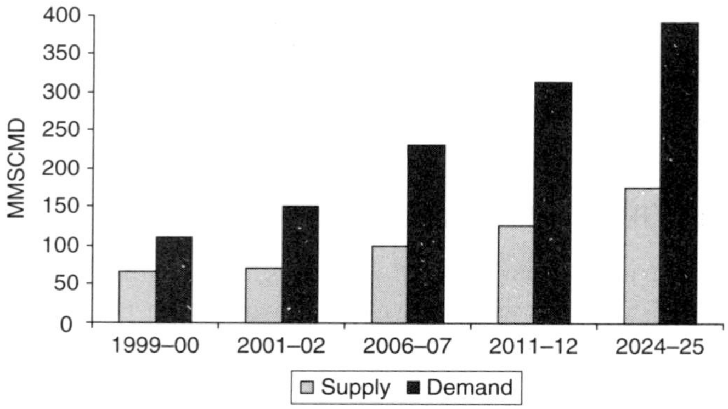

Source: *India Hydrocarbon Vision, 2025*

been able to meet 90 per cent of its total-energy needs indigenously. This has largely been possible because of the massive coal reserves of China (similar to India). Coal meets 70 per cent of China's energy requirements (55 per cent in India's case), and for both countries continues to be the cheapest and most competitive source of power generation. In fact, until 1993, halfway into its economic reforms, China was a net exporter of hydrocarbons.

In Beijing, more recent emphasis is being placed on energy conservation (target to cut per capita energy demand by 20 per cent over the next five years), and the use of technology to ease supply constrains and mitigate negative environmental consequences of energy use. Therein lies a policy lesson for India's policy planners and industry, as they deliberate a comprehensive energy-security strategy, beyond oil and gas! Tangentially, there is a strong argument for both Sino–Indian and multilateral cooperation to ensure the rapid adoption of clean-coal technologies for both these energy-hungry economies[38].

India's insecurity stems from three factors:

1. In the energy spectrum, it is the hydrocarbon resources that have multiple sources of user demand—transport (land, sea, and air) fuels, rural fuels, electricity generation (industrial and household)—that makes this component especially relevant from a security perspective.

2. Growing import dependence (75 per cent to 78 per cent compared to 46 per cent for China), translates to vulnerability. Additionally, lack of sufficient diversification in India (60 per cent imports from the Middle East) questions the reliability of these imports under different geopolitical futures. Finally, sustained, recent price increases have imposed

an additional financial burden through affordability. India's oil-import bill has gone up from US$ 26 billion in 2005 to US$ 40 billion in 2006.[39] Moreover, given the structural dynamic in global demand and supply, crude prices are unlikely to abate in the medium term.

3. India is the fourth largest producer of coal in the world next only to China, the USA and Australia, and is host to some of the largest reserves of coal in the world. It is estimated that it has more than 92,000 million tonnes that could last for the next 229 years at the current consumption levels. Coal further provides for 73 per cent of power generation in India. Yet, coal's logistical and environmental inefficiency along with a very weak policy environment further exacerbates India's energy dilemma. According to a recent KPMG report, in the absence of fresh investments, India's *mineable* coal reserves will be exhausted in 40 years.[40] See Chart 2.13.

DEFENCE EXPENDITURE

According to estimates of the US Defence Intelligence Agency (DIA), China's military spending in 2006 is projected to be in the range of US$ 70–105 billion, while the official Chinese CPC government defence-budget figure is US$ 35.6 billion. The actual Chinese military capabilities and budget are shrouded in deep secrecy. Nonetheless, even the official Chinese numbers make it the world's second-largest military spender. A December 2006 white paper released by Beijing states that from 1990 to 2005, average annual expenditure on defence registered a 15.36 per cent growth rate (10 per cent real annual average growth rate).

On the other side, India's official military spending was quoted at US$ 22 billion for 2006 by the Ministry of Finance (India) Budget (2006–2007).

Chart 2.13   India's Energy Mix

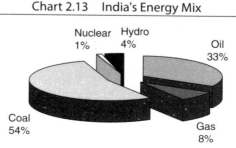

Source: Authors' estimates

India however, does not keep a level of secrecy as cloaked as China, primarily because of its democratic-government system and public accountability. As per its official 2006 military budget figures, India occupies the ninth position in global military spending. From 1991 to 2007, India's defence expenditure as a percentage of GDP has remained in the range of 2.0 per cent to 2.5 per cent. Defence expenditure as a percentage of total Central government expenditure has averaged 15 per cent over the past five years. The Indian budgeted defence expenditure (DE) for the year 2007–08 was Rs 96,000 crore and the Indian Army's share of this pie was approximately 47 per cent.

The projections of defence expenditure, in both the countries, on the existing basis illustrate the higher capacity of China to spend on defence. Thus, the projection for 2020 in China is US$ 96.60 billion, whereas India's is US$ 37.40 billion. The projection for 2050 shows the defence expenditure of China touching US$ 775 billion, while India's is expected to be US$ 215 billion or less than one-third of China (see Table 2.23 and Table 2.24).

Taking 2.4 per cent as the minimum benchmark and factoring a 10 per cent growth rate of China's GDP in 2006, the defence budget could be around US$ 60 billion in 2006 or three times higher than India's defence budget in 2006–07. Upgrading the benchmark to 3 per cent of GDP, China's defence budget stands at US$ 74 billion in the same year. Assuming 2.4 per cent of GDP is spent on defence and a minimum 10 per cent annual average growth in defence expenditure, China's defence budget will stand at US$ 97 billion at the end of five years and at US$ 155 billion at the end of 10 years from 2006. The figures will change to US$ 120 billion (5 years) and US$ 190 billion (10 years) if China spends 3 per cent of its GDP and the annual average growth of defence expenditure is kept at 10 per cent.[41]

Table 2.23   Defence Expenditure, 2004

Description	India	China
% of GDP	2.3	1.9
Real Exp. (US$ bn)*	11.9	26.6
Military Pers. (M)	2.61	3.75

Source: *World Development Indicators, 2006*
*Figure Pertains to 2000

Table 2.24   Defence Expenditure Projections (US$ billion)

Country	2000	2020	2050
India	11.95	37.40	215.17
China	26.65	96.60	774.47

Source: *World Development Indicators, 2005*

CLOSING THE GAP: FOCUSED SPENDING VIA INSTITUTIONAL REFORM

Currently, the National Security Council (NSC) and its support groups— the strategic policy group (SPG) and the national security advisory board (NSAB)—make periodic reviews of the domestic and external security concerns. Yet, there is an absence of an institutionalized arrangement despite calls to publish a comprehensive, strategic defence review.[42]

India can, therefore, draw lessons from China's publication of its white paper. A defence white paper, by appraising current and emerging security threats from a holistic politico-military and military-strategic perspective, would assign goals that would transcend bureaucratic politics. For instance, the current focus on simply bridging capability gaps needs to be transformed towards a long-term oriented strategy for the envisaged role that the armed forces would play in the potential application or exploitation of force. Further, once goals are deliberated and set, this would enable the focused financial allocations linked to economic benchmarks. Finally, periodic publication of white papers would allow timely readjustments via risk assessments.[43]

In nominal terms, though the economy grew by more than 45 per cent between 2004–05 and 2007–08, the defence budget has actually gone up by only 26 per cent in the same period (see Chart 2.14). Thus, the recommendation of the parliamentary standing committee on defence in its 16th report (April 2007) states:

> The Committee therefore, strongly recommends that the Ministry of Defence should take up the matter with the Ministry of Finance for providing a minimum 3 per cent of GDP for defence services every year in order to ensure a fixed amount to carry out their modernisation, capital acquisition, and R&D programmes and fulfil the need based requirements of the defence forces.[44]

Chart 2.14   India's Defence Budget as Per Cent of GDP

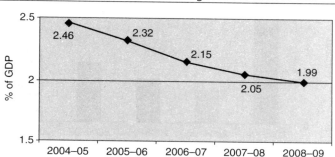

Source: CSO and RBI for GDP figures; DSE for Defence figures.

A caveat however, suggests that absorption of funds by the services could be a vital factor in the mismatch between defence spending and higher GDP growth rates. For instance, the defence services estimates (DSE) reveal that the armed forces have surrendered nearly Rs 40,000 crore in the past decade.[45]

Thus, perhaps, addressing the sub-optimal acquisition structure is a necessary objective in itself. First, the formulation of qualitative requirements (QRs) of weapons/platforms/systems is one of the most critical aspects of defence acquisition and has a strong bearing on defence capability and costs. QR formulation is intricately linked to various other acquisition functions such as solicitation of offers, trials and evaluations, etc. Thus, an inefficient QR makes vendor response restrictive and the trial and evaluation process time consuming, subjective, and uncompetitive. The QRs are still found to be narrow, unrealistic, inconsistent with the available technology, and worse, are anti-indigenization and vendor-specific. This has led to sub-optimal use of resources and time overruns (see Chart 2.15). Second, the handling of complex defence acquisition worth several thousand crores of rupees without proper expertise and by a set of scattered bodies (i.e., IDS for planning, DRDO for R&D, Armed Forces for QRs, DGQA for quality assurance and test and evaluations) implies an incoherent framework relative to international standards in major weapon-producing countries. In sum, India needs to emulate the best practices globally by adopting an integrated structure that includes all the key stakeholders—armed-forces industry, R&D organization, quality assurance organization, civilian bureaucrats—to avoid the 'numerous approvals and submission points' and

Chart 2.15   Underutilization of Capital Expenditure

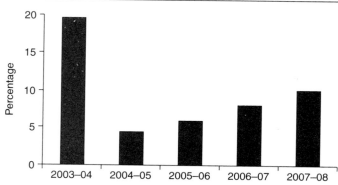

Source: DSE and Union Budget, various years

create a single point of accountability in the otherwise disparate bureaucratic chain.[46]

The Indian budgeted defence expenditure (DE) for the year 2007–08 was Rs 96,000 crore. However, when the expenditure on nuclear defence and the defence component of rupee debt on the rouble account payable to Russia, at least Rs 25,000 crore being spent on defence is not being budgeted as defence expenditure. The aggregate defence expenditure by the Indian government can thus be estimated at Rs 122,000 crore, or approximately 2.8 per cent of GDP. See Chart 2.16 below for the service-wise shares of defence budget for 2007–08.

The following revenue–capital break up of the latest defence budget in Table 2.25 is perhaps more useful when viewing India's defence spending in terms of modernization progress versus replacement spending.[47] Defence R&D constitutes barely 6 per cent of the total defence budget. Moreover, according to the defence ministry, the primary agency responsible for defence R&D—the Defence Research and Development Organization (DRDO)—a total of 1,107 scientists, mostly young entrants, have resigned from the DRDO between 2003 and 2007, an average of one person leaving every two days.

On the whole, India's autonomous capabilities in manufacturing critical military technologies and weapon platforms remain far too short of an aspiring regional power. India's self-reliance index of 30 per cent against the target of 70 per cent (end of 10th Plan) reveals the extent of India's import dependence on the conventional weapon systems. It may suffice to say that India's economic-development goals and the prevailing military technical asymmetry with the major powers, especially the United States and Russia, implies that

Chart 2.16   Service-wise Shares of Defence Budget, 2007–2008

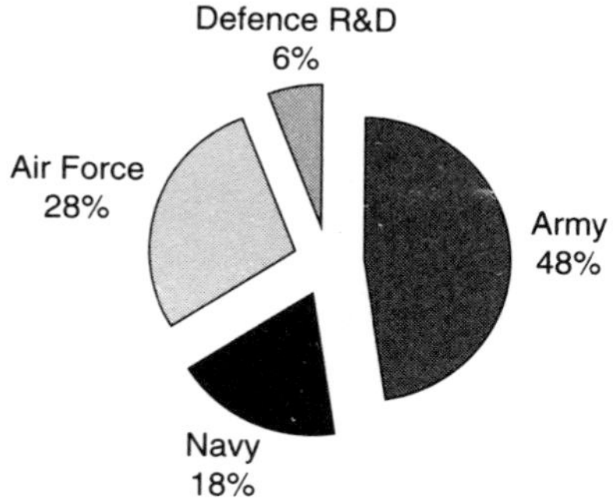

Defence R&D 6%

Air Force 28%

Army 48%

Navy 18%

Source: Laxman Kumar Behera, 'Indian Defence Acquisition: Time for Change', *IDSA Strategic Comments*, 3 August 2007, www.idsa.in.

Table 2.25   Revenue and Capital Ratios, 2007–2008

	Revenue (%)	Capital (%)
Army	74	26
Navy	40	60
Air force	38	62
Total	56	44

Source: Laxman Kumar Behera, 'Indian Defence Acquisition: Time for Change', *IDSA Strategic Comments*, 3 August 2007, www.idsa.in.

India's deterrence strategy must rely more on strategic weapons development rather than getting lured into an expensive conventional arms race.

GLOBAL TRENDS IN MILITARY SPENDING

Global military expenditure and the arms trade form the largest spending in the world, at over one trillion dollars in annual expenditure and have been rising in recent years (see Chart 2.17). According to Stockholm International Peace Research Institute (SIPRI), the concentration of military expenditure is:

Chart 2.17   World Military Expenditure

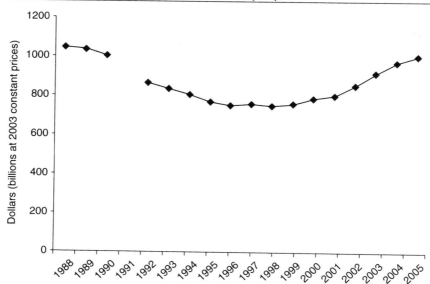

Source: *Stockholm International Peace Research Institute Yearbook 2006*

- The 15 countries with the highest spending account for 84 per cent of the total

- The USA is responsible for 48 per cent of the world total, distantly followed by the UK, France, Japan and China with 4 per cent to 5 per cent each (see Chart 2.18).

DEMOGRAPHY: A WINDOW OF OPPORTUNITY FOR INDIA?

China's population, in terms of age break up, is passing through a phase of great demographic advantage. The cohort in the productive phase (15–60 years) of the life cycle is at its peak, whereas, the dependency ratio in India is, relatively speaking, somewhat adverse (see Chart 2.19). While 64 per cent of China's population currently falls in the productive cohort, the corresponding figure for India is 59 per cent. However, in 20 years from now, while China's productive population will stagnate at 64 per cent India's productive cohort will rise to 64 per cent and hence, catch up with China. Moreover, the picture will further change by 2050 with India (61 per cent) overtaking China (55 per cent). This transformation is, however, not just limited to percentage terms, but is more importantly also palpable in absolute terms, as India would have become the most populous country in the world with 1.6 billion. This will be discussed in some greater detail in Chapter 7.

Chart 2.18   Military Expenditure Increase, 1996–2005

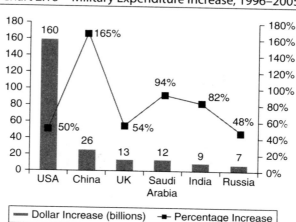

Source: *SIPRI Year Book 2006*

Table 2.26   Youth Illiteracy Rate in India and China

	Age 15–24	(Male %)	Age 15–24	(Female %)
Country	1990	2002	1990	2002
India	27	16	46	32
China	3	1	7	1

Source: *World Development Indicators, 2006*

Table 2.27   Population in Productive Cohort (M)

	2000	2020	2050
China	812	921	824
India	599	824	962

Sources: United Nations; World Bank

Thus, while at present, China's productive population stands at a whopping 812 million, and India's seemingly way behind at 599 million, by 2050, India's productive population will be a huge 962 million and China would be behind at 824 million (see Table 2.27 and Chart 2.19). But whether India will be able to convert this into an economic advantage is still to be seen. That entails India tooling up to create a more productive and able workforce, stimulate investments and create a much bigger market for goods and services.

This favourable demographic trend is as much a window of opportunity as it is a potential liability.[48] According to a 2003 study of population projections for major states[49], the four BIMARU states' (Bihar, Madhya Pradesh, Rajasthan and Uttar Pradesh) share of India's population will rise from

Chart 2.19   Population in Productive Cohort

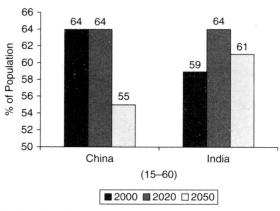

(15–60)

■ 2000 ■ 2020 ☐ 2050

Source: United Nations, World Bank

41 per cent in 2001 to 48 per cent in 2051. Thus, 60 per cent of India's population increment will be concentrated in these four states. Thus, as Acharya notes, with these four 'populous, poor, slow-growing northern states with weak infrastructure, education systems, and governance', the prospects of translating this 'demographic dividend' into a 'reality of employment and high growth remain slim'.[50]

As noted earlier, the public share of overall educational expenditure of both China and India remains the same in recent years. The major drawback in the Indian case is that it does not translate into endowment of human capital because of structural flaws that stifle the delivery process. The higher incidence of youth illiteracy in India amply illustrates that. The youth male illiteracy in India was 20 times higher than that of China in the year 2002. Likewise, the female youth illiteracy remained at 32 per cent, a contrast to China with 1 per cent of its female youths remaining illiterate in the year 2002 (see Table 2.26).

There is another interesting dimension, which has socio-economic consequences. A recent study has shown that it is the 'restless' workers that make an economy volatile. Based on historical data from the major industrial countries, the study finds that volatility of an economy is positively correlated with the share of young workers (15–29 years old) in the labour force.[51] Thus, that India's demographic change may impose additional business-cycle volatility should further alert Indian policy planners.

Nonetheless, if India grasps the opportunity by investing in physical and human capital, it can elevate itself to a much higher level of prosperity. On the other hand, if India fails to do so, it will move into a period of unfavourable demographic distribution where it will be saddled with a rapidly greying population that will act as a natural brake against fast economic growth. China has so far successfully seized this opportunity, but will India follow suit?

NOTES

1   'Push for Power Reforms', *Tribune News Service*, 26 February 2005, www.tribuneindia.com.

2   'Sectoral Real Growth Rates of GDP (at factor cost)', *Economic Survey*, 2004–05, Government of India, General Review, p. 3.

3   Planning Commission, 2007.

4   Shankar Acharya, 'Governance and Health', *Business Standard*, 30 August 2007. Article available on this link-http://www.business-standard.com/india/storypage.php?autono=296267.

5   Jean Drèze and Amartya Sen, 'India and China' in *India: Economic Development and Social Opportunity*, New Delhi: Oxford University Press, 1995.

6   Calculated using CAGR formula $A = P\{(1 + R)^\wedge N\}$.

7   Source: Ministry of Finance, *Economic & Functional Classification of the Central Government Budget*—various issues.

8   Source: 'Expenditure on Wages and Salary', *Economic Survey 2006–07*; 'State Finances a Study of Budgets 2006–07', RBI and Budget 2006–07.

9   Unless indicated otherwise, estimates of the overstatement of FDI inflows into China are from Geng Xiao, *Round-Tripping Foreign Direct Investment in the People's Republic of China: Scale, Causes and Implications*, Asian Development Bank Institute Discussion Paper No. 7, June 2004.

10   Alex Erskine, 'The Rise in China's FDI: Myths and Realities', Australia-China Free Trade Agreement Conference, Sydney, 12–13 August 2004, www.apec.org.

11   For a detailed discussion on this, see Subramaniam Swamy, *Economic Reforms and Performance: China and India in Comparative Perspective*, Delhi: Konark Publishers, 2003.

12   T. Ram Mohan, 'Are FDI Flows into India for Real?', *The Economic Times*, 4 October 2007.

13   China's FDI-related issues and its geo-economic implications are discussed in subsequent chapters.

14   Aseema Sinha, 'Ideas, Interests, and Institutions in Policy Change: A Comparison of West Bengal and Gujarat', in Rob Jenkins (ed.), *Regional Reflections Comparing Politics Across India's States* (2004), New Delhi: Oxford University Press, 2004, p. 3.

15   Ibid, p. 3.

16   Ibid, p. 55.

17   Aseema Sinha, *The Regional Roots of Developmental Politics in India: A Divided Leviathan*, Indiana:, Indiana University Press, 2005, pp. 88, 263–64.

18   Carl Dahlman and Anuja Utz, *India and the Knowledge Economy: Leveraging Strengths and Opportunities*, World Bank, July 2005.

19   'China will Become the World's Second Highest Investor in R&D by End of 2006, Finds OECD', OECD press release, 4 Dec 2006, www.oecd.org.

20   'China Needs Innovation, OECD Says', *International Herald Tribune*, 27 August 2007.

21   *The Atlas of Ideas: Mapping the New Geography of Science*, DEMOS, 2007.

22   Dominic Wilson and Roopa Purushothaman, *Dreaming with the BRICs: The Path to 2050*, Global Economics Paper No. 99, Goldman Sachs, 1 October 2003, p. 14.

23   The seven IITs have an enrolment of 30,000 students, about as many as a single state university campus in the United States.

24 Devesh Kapur and Sunil Khilnani, 'Primary Concerns', *Hindustan Times*, 23 April 2006.

25 According to McKinsey (2005), only 25 per cent of engineers, 15 per cent of finance and accounting professionals and 10 per cent of professionals with degrees, in India, are suitable for work in multinational companies.

26 Philip G. Altbach, 'Tiny at the Top', *Wilson Quarterly*, Autumn 2006.

27 Devesh Kapur and Pratap Bhanu Mehta, 'Indian Higher Education Reform: From Half-Baked Socialism to Half-Baked Capitalism', CID Working Paper No. 108, Centre for International Development, Harvard University, September 2004, p. 14.

28 Ibid.

29 Carl Dahlman and Anuja Utz, *India and the Knowledge Economy: Leveraging Strengths and Opportunities*, World Bank, July 2005.

30 Ibid.

31 According to a 2006 consultation paper by the Ministry of Commerce, 'FDI could be used as an opportunity to invite foreign universities to set up campuses in India, thereby saving billions of dollars for the students travelling abroad.' Thus, by striking 'a balance' between 'domestic regulation and providing adequate flexibility to such Universities in setting syllabus, hiring teachers, screening students and setting fee levels', an environment conducive for private participation can be created.

32 'IEA Warns of "Supply Crunch" in Oil Despite High Prices', *International Herald Tribune*, 9 July 2007.

33 Mark Shenk, 'Emerging Market Oil Use Exceeds U.S. as Prices Rise', 21 April 2008, www.bloomberg.com,.

34 Erica Downs, 'China's Quest for Overseas Oil', *Far Eastern Economic Review*, September 2007.

35 'PetroChina to Buy Up to A$60 Billion of Australia LNG', 6 September 2007, www.bloomberg.com; Shai Oster, 'In China, a Domestic Shift Spurs New Approach on Natural Gas', *The Wall Street Journal*, 10 September 2007.

36 In 2006, Moscow signed a deal with Beijing, according to which it promised two pipelines to China: From West and East Siberia, to begin pumping gas through the west link in 2011 and by the east link in 2016.

37 'India Set to Engage Myanmar to Try and Snag More Gas Supply', *PTI*, 18 Sep 2007.

38 Jaspal Singh Sindharh, 'Energy: Confrontation or Cooperation?', *Saisphere*, Johns Hopkins University, 2006, http://www.sais-jhu.edu/pubaffairs/publications/saisphere/winter06/.

39 'Oil Import Bill Jumps to $40 b in April', www.sify.com, 10 April 2006.

40   'KPMG: India has to Pump $10 billion in Energy Sector', *Deccan Chronicle*, 4 April 2006.

41   Laxman Kumar Behera, 'China's Defence White Paper: Can India Draw Some Lessons?', *IDSA Strategic Comments*, 31 January 2007, www.idsa.in.

42   The exception is the MoD's *Rakhsa Mantri's Operational Directives*, which only serves the planning purpose of the Armed Forces.

43   Laxman Kumar Behera, 'China's Defence White Paper: Can India Draw Some Lessons?', *IDSA Strategic Comments*, 31 January 2007, www.idsa.in.

44   http://164.100.24.208/ls/committeeR/Defence/16threport.pdf.

45   Laxman Kumar Behera, 'The Indian Defence Budget 2007–08', *IDSA Strategic Comments*, 9 March 2007, www.idsa.in.

46   Laxman Kumar Behera, 'Indian Defence Acquisition: Time for Change', *IDSA Strategic Comments*, 3 August 2007, www.idsa.in.

47   http://www.indiabudget.nic.in/ub2007-08/eb/vol2.htm.

48   To exploit the demographic dividend, the population needs to be educated, trained and employable. Further, healthcare and food security are core human capital investments that will need to undertaken. For a critique of the demography dividends hypothesis, see Shankar Acharya, *Can India Grow Without Bharat?*, New Delhi: Academic Foundation, 2007, pp. 27–31.

49   Leela and Pravin Visaria, 'Long-term Population Projections for Major States, 1991–2101', *Economic and Political Weekly*, November 2003.

50   Acharya (2007), p. 30.

51   Nir Jaimovich and Henry E. Siu, 'The Young, the Old, and the Restless: Demographics and Business Cycle Volatility', *NBER Working Papers 14063*, National Bureau of Economic Research, 2008.

FDI in China: A Brief Survey

3

EVOLUTION OF CHINA'S FOREIGN INVESTMENT POLICY

It has been three decades since Chairman Deng uttered the words: 'It's glorious to be rich' and 'it does not matter whether the cat is black or white, as long as it catches the mice!' This was the signal to throw overboard the Marxist-Leninist orthodoxy and Maoist idiosyncrasies. Following these fundamental changes, which were initiated at the third plenary session of the 11th Chinese Communist Party Congress in December 1978, began the wave of revolutionary reforms that have since transformed the Chinese economy. China has attracted a spectacular amount of FDI since it opened up to the outside world in 1979 (see Chart 3.1). Average FDI inflows rose from US$ 3.9 billion in 1985–1992 to US$ 37.8 billion in 1993–2000 and to US$ 59 billion for 2001–2006. FDI inflows are forecast to remain high, averaging US$ 87 billion in 2007–2011[1] (see Chart 3.2). In twenty-four years (1979–2003), the FDI stocks of China increased to US$ 501.7 billion, which is equivalent to 6.1 per cent of direct investment worldwide.[2] The stock of inward FDI reached US$ 700 billion by end-2006, making China the fifth-highest recipient in accumulated flows.[3]

Chinese FDI trends can be distinguished according to the changes in policy directions—first phase: 1979–83, second phase: 1984–91, and third phase: 1992–99.

Phase I (1979–83): The enactment of the Equity Joint Venture Law (Sino-foreign joint ventures) in July 1979, the first of its kind, formally opened up China's market to the world. The law provided the legal framework for foreign investors to form equity joint ventures with their Chinese partners with a commitment that the state would not nationalize or expropriate foreign investment interest.[4] Subsequently, in August 1980, four special economic zones (SEZs) were established in Guangdong and Fujian provinces, and offered special incentive policies for FDI in these SEZs. While FDI inflows into China were highly concentrated in these SEZs, the amount was rather limited. The total inflows of realized FDI during these five years

Chart 3.1   FDI Inflows, 1979–2011

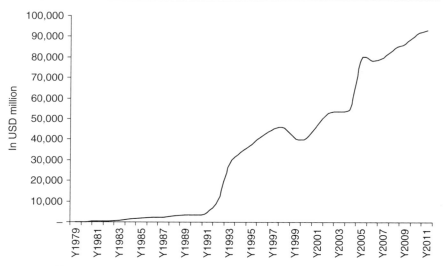

Source: *World Investment Report 2004*, UNCTAD; Data for 2004–2011 from the Economist Intelligence Unit (*World Investment Prospects to 2001*) www.eiu.com

Chart 3.2   Leading FDI Recipients, 2007–2011 (FDI Inflows, Annual Average)

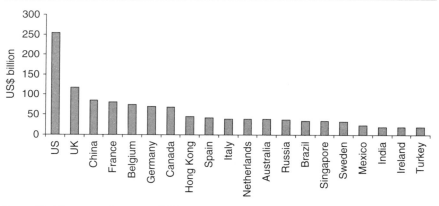

Source: *World Investment Prospects to 2011*
Emerging markets accounted for 38 per cent of total world FDI inflows in 2006 (US$ 1.3 trillion).
See Chart 3.3

amounted to only US$ 1.8 billion, averaging US$ 360 million annually. It is interesting, as a later chapter will note that the reform policy had a bias toward the south-eastern coastal region, which has contributed to a geographic concentration of FDI in the eastern region.

Chart 3.3   Top Emerging-market FDI Recipients, 2006

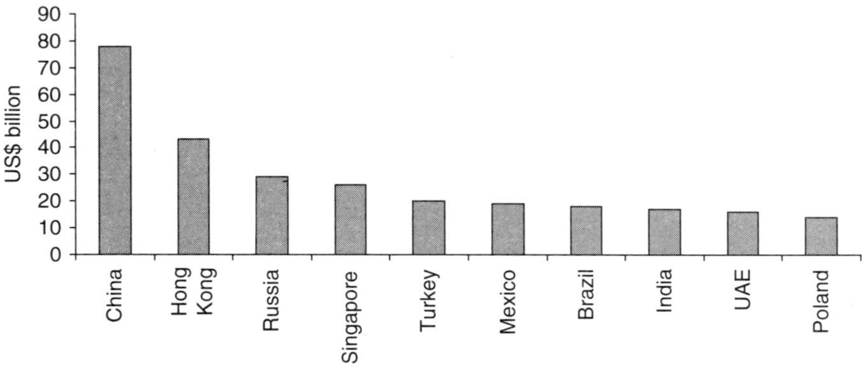

Source: *World Investment Prospects to 2011*, Economist Intelligence Unit

The establishment of the SEZs had five objectives, which are summarized below:[5]

- To develop the coastal area of China through experimental, controlled enclaves

- To attract and exploit foreign investment

- To promote export-led growth, create local employment, and generate foreign exchange

- To serve as 'policy laboratories', where policies could be tested, which if successful, could be adopted elsewhere in China

- To enhance the link of Hong Kong, Macao, and Taiwan with mainland China and to serve as China's window to the outside world

Phase II (1984–91): In 1984, fourteen more coastal cities and Hainan Island were opened to foreign investment. During this year, these cities soon established their own economic and technological development zones (ETDZs) and a variety of favourable treatments were adopted to encourage foreign business. Three more zones were opened to FDI in early 1985—the Yangtze River delta, the Pearl River delta, and the Zhangzhou–Quanzhou–Xiamen region. FDI, hence, spread out from the SEZs but the boom ended in late 1985 due to high inflation. During this stage, the majority of FDI inflow came mainly from Hong Kong and Macau, with investments concentrated in small-sized assembling and processing units for exports. Total FDI inflows amounted to US$ 10.3

during the period 1984–88, with an annual average of US$ 2.1 billion. However, despite the investments from Hong Kong and Macau, the overall performance of foreign-capital inflow was insignificant and did not meet the expectation of the reform process. There were several factors behind this disappointment:[6]

- The legal environment for foreign investors was not well-defined
- There was a lack of communications-and-transport-infrastructure development
- There was a shortage of skilled labour

In response to a decline in FDI, the government promulgated the PRC law on foreign enterprises in April 1986; formally granting legal rights to wholly owned foreign enterprises in China. In October 1986, the State Council further issued the 'Provisions for the Encouragement of Foreign Investment' permitting more freedom of independent operations for foreign-invested enterprises (FIEs)[7] and granting more tax incentives for foreign investment. More decentralization followed, as local governments were also given more authority in reviewing the applications of foreign investment. These key changes have now come to be known as the 'twenty-two regulations'.

The Tiananmen Square incident slowed down the FDI growth rate to a single digit in 1989 and 1990, which ended this second stage of FDI development.

Phase III (1992–99): The seminal phase began in the spring of 1992, when Deng Xiaoping toured China's southern coastal areas and SEZs, which was accompanied by the declaration of the 14th Party Congress that China was to pursue a 'socialist market economy.' His visit, which intended mainly to push China's overall economic reform process forward and to emphasize China's commitment to the open-door policy and market-oriented economic reform, proved to be a success in garnering the confidence of foreign investors in China. Consequently, China adopted a new approach, which turned away from special regimes toward a more nation-wide implementation of open policies for FDI.

Following Deng Xiaoping's South China tour, actual FDI surged by 150 per cent to US$ 11 billion in 1992. It surged another 150 per cent in 1993 and maintained the double-digit growth thereafter. In the 1980s, FDI mainly took the form of contractual or equity joint ventures. However, the wholly owned foreign firm was the fastest growing form of FDI in the 1990s.

It accounted for 40 per cent of the FDI value in 1996. The average capital size of FDI increased, with the main focus shifting to large infrastructure and manufacturing projects. The fourth key change came with China's entry into the WTO at the Doha Ministerial meeting in 2001.[8] Following the WTO entry, China attracted a record of US\$ 52.7 billion in foreign direct investment in 2002.

THE DATA

FDI into China takes two forms—market-accessing investment and investment for export production. The latter dominates FDI into China, accounting for at least two-thirds of all FDI. Until China's WTO entry, China ran a dualistic trade regime, with a relatively closed and protected domestic market and a relatively liberal export-promotion regime.

The importance of FDI for China's economy up to early 2000 is clearly evident from the trend in Chart 3.4. The relative measure (FDI stock/GDP) shows that China's dependence increased through the 1990s, but by 2004, the ratio had peaked at 28 per cent, and is now declining. In 2007, the ratio was 24 per cent.

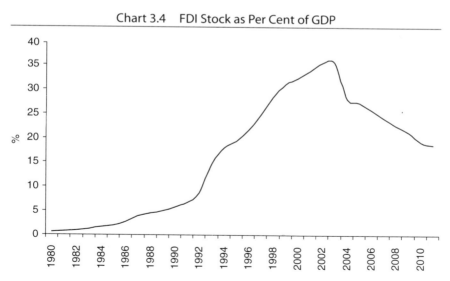

Chart 3.4   FDI Stock as Per Cent of GDP

Source: *World Investment Report, 2004*, UNCTAD; Data for 2004–2011 from the Economist Intelligence Unit (*World Investment Prospects to 2001*)

FDI INFLOWS IN COMPARISON WITH OTHER CAPITAL SOURCES

The average share of FDI inflows as a percentage of gross fixed-capital formation (GFCF) has averaged around 7 per cent in the period 1979–2003. The figure increased sharply in 1992 when the 'high growth phase' started and peaked in 1995 to around 17 per cent of GFCF (see Chart 3.5). The FDI/GFCF is now falling and is forecast to be at 5.5 per cent for the period 2004–2011.[9]

Overall, China has seen a twenty-fold increase in capital inflows from the early 1980s to 1998. The aggregate capital inflows into China grew steadily during the 1980s, but they have increased very rapidly since the early 1990s, which was overwhelmingly led by the large inflows of FDI. Among the three forms of capital inflows—foreign direct investment, external loans, and other foreign investment—the shares of these flows have changed gradually from the 1980s to the 1990s. During the 1980s, capital inflows into China were dominated by external loans, accounting for around 60 per cent of China's total capital inflows. Since 1992, however, the inflows of FDI surpassed external loans and have been the dominant source of capital inflows, accounting for around 70 per cent of the total capital inflows. Other foreign investment, which includes foreign portfolio investment and international leasing,

Chart 3.5   FDI Inflows as Per Cent Gross Fixed Capital Formation

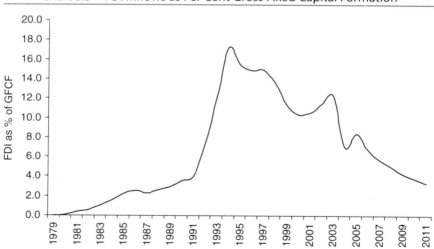

Source: *World Investment Report, 2004*, UNCTAD; Data for 2004–2011 from Economist Intelligence Unit (*World Investment Prospects to 2001*)

accounted for only 4.8 per cent of the total capital inflows into China during the period from 1979 to 2000, and its annual share in the total capital inflows has been declining since then.[10]

Gross domestic capital formation in Chart 3.5 is inclusive of investments by state-owned enterprises SOEs. Given the large public sector in China's economy, it could be useful to isolate the private sector investment. The FDI/capital formation ratio net of investments by the public sector reveals China's high FDI dependency. By this measure, for the period 1992–1998, China's FDI/capital formation ratio was 27.9 per cent.[11]

GEOGRAPHICAL DISTRIBUTION OF FDI

Nearly 90 per cent of cumulative FDI since 1978 has gone to China's coastal provinces. Since the initiation of reforms, China has implemented an unbalanced, regional, economic-development strategy with the eastern region as the priority of state investment.[12] The eastern region has traditionally contributed the most to China's GDP and recent statistics reveal that this is still the case, although, inner China is contributing more to economic development (see Chart 3.6). And the FDI inflow reflects the relative importance of these regions and an overwhelming concentration of FDI in the east (see Chart 3.7).

FDI inflows in the 1990s have diffused from the initially concentrated southern coastal areas towards the south-eastern and eastern coastal areas as well as towards inland areas (see Chart 3.8). The three provincial groups of the eastern, central and western regions experienced different patterns in FDI inflows. For the eastern-region provinces, FDI inflows have been increasing steadily with a remarkably high growth rate, particularly from 1992 to 1998. For the other two provincial groups, the inflows of FDI have been much less, especially for the western-region provinces. As a result, the gap between the eastern region and the central and western regions in terms of the absolute magnitude of annual FDI inflows has actually broadened since 1992.[13]

Chart 3.6   As a Proportion of China's Total GDP in 2002

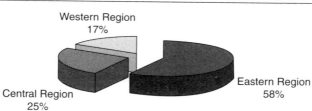

Western Region
17%

Central Region
25%

Eastern Region
58%

Source: *China Foreign Investment Report, 2003*

Chart 3.7   Realized Foreign Investment as a Per Cent of Total FDI Inflow in 2002

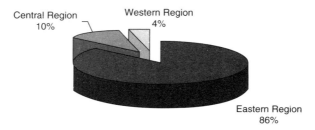

Source: *China Foreign Investment Report, 2003*

Chart 3.8   Cumulative FDI into Eastern Provinces and Municipalities
by End of 2002

Eastern Region's FDI stock: USD 377 Billion

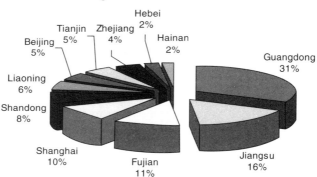

Source: *China Foreign Investment Report, 2003*

One reason is that the general efficiency of the labour force is higher in the coastal areas than it is in the central and western areas.[14]

THE TREND (see Chart 3.9 and Table 3.1)

- **Hong Kong**: Investment in the mainland reached a historic high in 1993. Between 1986 and 2002, the share of Hong Kong's investment in the mainland displayed a downward trend indicative of the diversification of the sources of investment.

- **Taiwan**: Between 1989 and 2002, Taiwan's share of total FDI increased from 4.5 per cent to 7.5 per cent in 2002, but dropped to 4 per cent by 2005.

- **USA**: Between 1986 and 2002, the USA's share of total FDI has decreased from 14.5 per cent to 10.2 per cent in 2002, and to 5 per cent

Chart 3.9   Main Countries of Origin, FDI, 2005

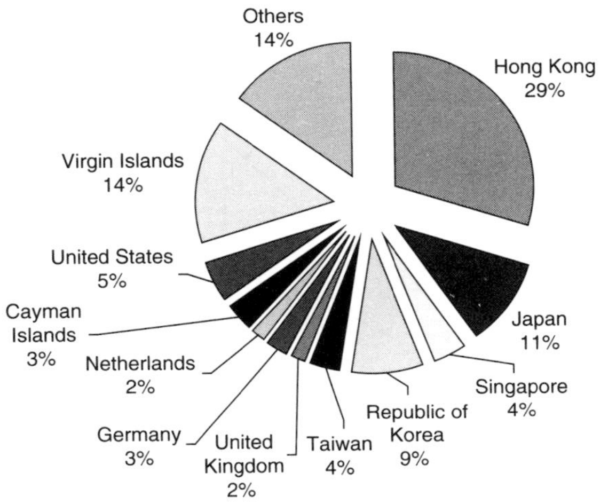

Source: *China Statistical Yearbook, 2006*

Table 3.1   Major Investors, 1979–2005

Country	USD Billion	% of Total
Total	632.8	100
Hong Kong	259.5	41.8
Japan	53.3	8.6
United States	51.1	8.2
British Virgin Islands	45.9	7.4
Taiwan	41.8	6.7
South Korea	31.1	5.0

Source: *China Statistical Yearbook*, various issues

by 2005. (Of course, investment via offshore islands would increase US share.)

- **Japan**: Japan's share, which decreased from 11.7 per cent in 1986 to 7.9 per cent in 2002, again regained an 11 per cent share.
- **Virgin Islands**: Since 1991, the free port Virgin Islands, 'a tax haven', has been the source of active investment in China. From a negligible share in 1992, it had increased its share to 11.6 per cent in 2002.
- **Singapore**: Its share has risen from 0.61 per cent in 1986 to 4.4 per cent in 2002, and it has maintained its share.
- **South Korea**: Since 1992, Korean direct investment has grown faster than the national average. Its share has increased from 1 per cent in 1992 to 5.16 per cent in 2002, and rapidly increased to 9 per cent by 2005.

Chart 3.10   Foreign-invested Enterprises: Contribution to Trade

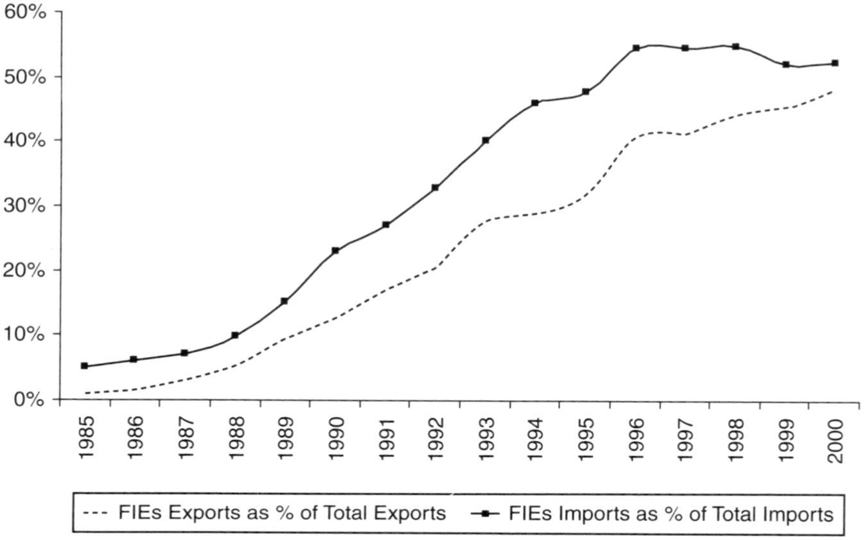

--- FIEs Exports as % of Total Exports   ▬■▬ FIEs Imports as % of Total Imports

Source: Nicholas Lardy, *Integrating China into the Global Economy*, Washington, DC: Brookings Institution Press, 2002, p. 7.

That FDI has been primarily export-oriented is clearly evident from Chart 3.10. By 2000, the foreign-invested firms, which accounted for only about one-eighth of all manufacturing output, were responsible for almost one-half of all of China's exports and imports.

FDI AS A SIGN OF WEAKNESS: A CONTRARIAN'S VIEW

Yasheng Huang, an economist at the Massachusetts Institute of Technology (MIT) in a recent book[15] has portrayed some interesting perspectives, which challenge the conventional wisdom in the existing FDI literature on China. His central claim is that the large absorption of FDI by China is a sign of some substantial distortions in its economic and financial system, and to understand China's FDI patterns, one must discern the larger institutional and economic contexts of the 1990s.

These economic and financial distortions have led to a weak domestic corporate sector, despite more than 20 years of continuous economic and export growth. FDI surged in part because of strong economic growth but also because of the failings of the domestic corporate sector to respond to and capitalize on the favourable macro conditions. The reason for the non-competitiveness of domestic firms is that China's product and capital market is extremely fragmented. This market fragmentation constrains the domestic firms more than the foreign firms, by allowing foreign firms to expand investments and to respond to market opportunities relative to domestic firms. According to Huang, the preceding decade should be divided into two periods—pre-1997 and post-1997; while, in the former period, FDI rose because internal reform was lacking, the latter period has witnessed a fundamental shift in the pace and scale of China's internal reforms. Since 1997, FDI has played a relatively less important role in China's economy.

According to Huang, FDI patterns are intricately linked to the Chinese domestic corporate sector, particularly its banking sector. The banking sector, whose role is to allocate domestic savings, has been completely dedicated to financing the SOEs, which were given a privileged position in China's economic development.[16] At the same time, FIEs were afforded a superior legal status compared with domestic firms.[17] This political pecking order with domestic, private firms at the bottom created a 'lending bias', which deprived the non-state corporate sector of investment funds. This unique scenario resulted in a 'demand pull' for foreign capital, which was readily absorbed by the private sector. So China, which has amongst the highest savings rate in the world,[18] still drew in huge foreign capital because indigenous savings were prevented from being channelled efficiently. Empirically, this seems to hold, as during the pre-1997 period, FDI increased, while domestic (private) investing was constrained, leading to a rising FDI/GFCF ratio (see Chart 3.11).

Chart 3.11   FDI Inflows as Per Cent Gross Fixed Capital Formation

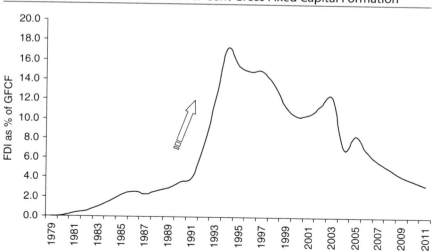

Source: *World Investment Report, 2004*, UNCTAD; Data for 2004–2011 from the Economist Intelligence Unit (*World Investment Prospects to 2001*)

The second explanation for high FDI is the structure of the Chinese economy, which is essentially one of a decentralized nature; each region is operationally and financially autonomous. Such an arrangement has led to the 'miniaturization' of Chinese firms, which cannot leverage on scale-economies by operating in the larger Chinese economy. This fragmentation has segmented markets for goods, services, and factors of production (for instance, labour restrictions as embodied in the *hukou* system have segregated urban and rural labour markets), which are not easily mobile across regions. This immobility, especially of domestic capital, has attracted foreign capital particularly in the remote, interior regions of China, where domestic companies were restricted from investing.

Since 1997, China has sped up internal reforms, particularly vis à vis domestic private companies. In 1997, the four largest state-owned banks were allowed to lend money to private companies. In 1999, for the first time, private domestic companies were also allowed to export directly. These reforms have led to dramatic changes in FDI inflows. The labour-intensive FDI has been reduced greatly, while high-tech FDI is increasing. The FDI is also becoming more concentrated in specific industries and there has been a striking rise in contractual exports. Taken together, these changes in the post-1997 period point to a more healthy Chinese economy and a higher quality of FDI. Huang's institutional model is more instructive for pre-1997 FDI. However, post-1997, the 'know-how' FDI is increasing.

Barry Naughton's analysis seems to be consistent with Huang's findings on economic fragmentation:

> Since these exports were assembled or processed from duty-free imported parts and components, their rapid growth created only a limited demand for inputs produced by domestic firms. Thus, a very large part of the export-producing sector could be seen as an enclave, with limited linkages to the rest of the domestic economy, which remained much more insulated from the international economy.[19]

Finally, in a comparative vein, India too has historically followed a system of control over the financial sector, where similar to China, the state was the primary user of household savings via a captive banking system, therefore, crowding out private firms. Thus, the structurally induced 'demand pull' logic of FDI was presumably strong. Yet, India (unlike China) was unable to implement appropriate liberalization measures to draw in FDI. This was further exacerbated by the lack of infrastructure and inflexible labour markets making India an unattractive destination as an export hub.

DEFINITION ISSUES AND CAVEATS

This section is added to highlight some of the recurring themes in the FDI literature on China—the emphasis on 'Chinese' investment into the PRC also known as 'round-tripping'.[20] The primary driver for round-tripping was the incentive of local capital to return disguised as foreign investment to avail of the preferential tax incentives, greater access to bank loans, and superior protection of property rights accorded to the foreign-invested enterprises. Since the late 1990s, as private firms were accorded equal status and greater access to domestic financing, the logic for round-tripping has certainly diminished.

Nonetheless, in recent years, the share of investment from the British Virgin Islands (now the second-largest investor) and the Cayman Islands (now eighth) has increased and the majority is widely accepted to originate in Hong Kong and Taiwan.

The process flow of round-tripping has been illustrated in Chart 3.12. Quantifying 'round-tripping' has been extremely difficult. A 2003 Deutsche Bank paper suggested a figure of 25 per cent.[21] Higher estimates put the figure for round-tripping at 50 per cent of the total FDI.[22] The World Bank reported that 25 per cent of all FDI from Hong Kong into China was round-tripping investment.[23] The example of recycled investment channelled through tax havens makes it hard to read bilateral investment figures. For instance, 'the number of companies in Hong Kong that are incorporated in Bermuda and the Cayman Islands jumped 5.2 times from 178 in 1990 to 924 in 2000'.[24]

What the investment figures don't tell us is the way in which extra-regional actors are engaging with the Chinese economy (discussed in Chapter 5). Enterprises in Hong Kong, Singapore, and Taiwan play a key role as intermediaries between China and the global political economy, suggesting that processes of regionalization are themselves often dependent on global processes. And given China's significant position in the global production value-chains

Chart 3.12   Round-tripping

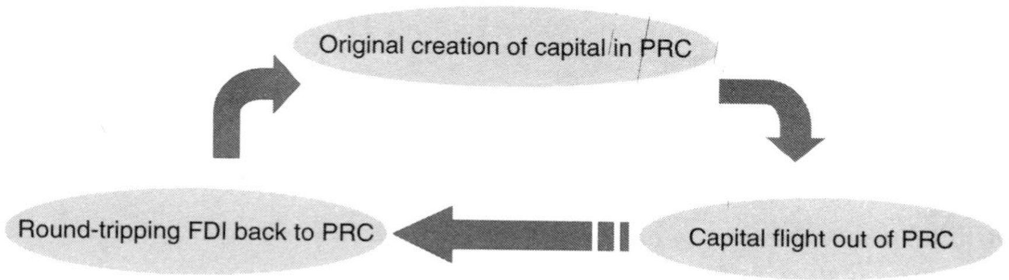

Original creation of capital in PRC

Capital flight out of PRC

Round-tripping FDI back to PRC

Chart 3.13   Inward FDI Stock, 2002–2011

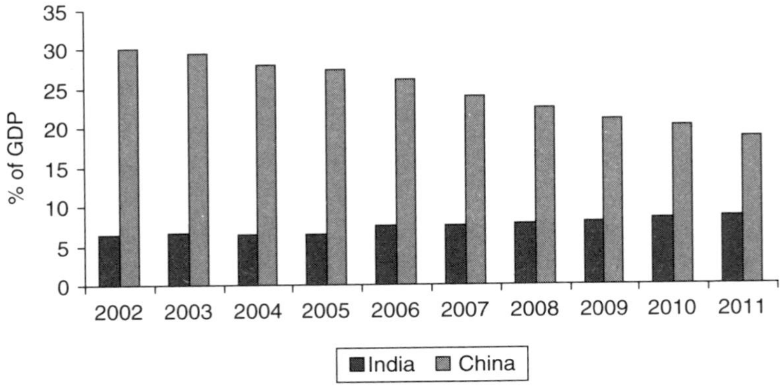

Source: The Economist Intelligence Unit (*World Investment Prospects to 2011*)

and the fact that many US and Japanese manufacturers' investment in China is through regional third parties, investment figures underplay the level of engagement these economies have with China. Therefore, the official and bilateral figures are only a rough guide to analyse the data, and as described above, can be misleading, given the variety of estimates available. Finally, FDI, as defined by China, is at the level of at least 25 per cent of a firm's equity compared to 10 per cent in OECD countries[25]. This suggests a downward bias in a cross-country comparison.

The FDI importance for India is growing gradually, while diminishing for China. However, given the GDP asymmetry, absolute foreign investment in China is likely to dwarf India's share (see Chart 3.13).

NOTES

1   'World Investment Prospects to 2011: Foreign Direct Investment and the Challenge of Political Risk'; Economist Intelligence Unit, 2007 (www.eiu.com).

2   According to UNCTAD's WIR 2004, the World FDI stock of inward investment in 2003 was USD 8.24 trillion.

3   'World Investment Prospects to 2011: Foreign Direct Investment and the Challenge of Political Risk', Economist Intelligence Unit & Columbia Program on International Investment, 2007.

4   Jun Fu, *Institutions and Investments: Foreign Direct Investment in China During an Era of Reforms*, Ann Arbor, MI: University of Michigan Press, 2000.

5   K. I. McKenney, *An Assessment of China's Special Economic Zones*, Washington, D.C: Industrial College of the Armed Forces, Fort Lesley J. McNair, 1993.

6   Wei Zhang, 'Why Is Foreign Investment Concentrated in the Coastal Areas?', *Harvard Asia Quarterly*, Summer 2000.

7   Foreign-invested enterprises, refers to firms in China with a foreign equity stake of at least 25 per cent.

8   In December 2001, China became the 143rd member of WTO.

9   op. cit., *World Investment Prospects to 2011, 2007*.

10 Despite the introduction of stock markets, and the ability of foreigners to buy B shares, the overwhelming majority of FDI is in productive capacity. The still relatively closed nature of the Chinese financial sector combined with the lack of currency convertibility makes portfolio investments both difficult and unattractive.

11 Yasheng Huang, *Selling China: Foreign Direct Investment During the Reform Era*, New York: Cambridge University Press, 2003.

12 In 2000, the Chinese government launched a 'Look West' strategy aimed at encouraging more investment into central and western China.

13 Between 1992 and 1998, interior regions of China received US$ 31.5 billion in FDI (13 per cent). In a comparative perspective, this is still a large number compared with India's entire FDI stock as of 1997 of US$ 11.2 billion or even the emerging economies of Latin America in the 1990s.

14 Wei Zhang argues that the preferential policies enjoyed by the coastal provinces in China are not the fundamental reasons for the spectacular growth in these areas since reform. Instead, the main driving forces are their inherent comparative advantages.

15 Op. cit., Yasheng Huang, 2003.

16 The legal and regulatory restrictions on the private sector, which subordinated them to the state sector, were embodied in the Chinese Constitution. It was not until March 1999 that the Chinese Constitution recognized the private sector as an integral part of the economy and assigned it an equal footing with other firms.

17 In the 1982 Constitution.

18 Between 1986 and 1992, the Chinese savings rate was 36 per cent, and between 1994 and 1997, it rose to 42 per cent (State Statistical Bureau).

19 Barry Naughton, 'China's Emergence and Prospects as a Trading Nation', *Economic Studies Program*, Volume 27, Brookings Papers on Economic Activity, 1996.

20 UNCTAD referred to this process as 'transit FDI' in the 2001 *World Investment Report*.

21   Manu Bhaskaran, 'China as Potential Superpower: Regional Responses', *Deutsche Bank Research Report,* 15 January 2003.

22   K. Subramanian, 'FDI: Any Lessons from China?', *The Hindu*, 18 November 2002.

23   *Global Development Finance 2002*, World Bank, 2002. The Bank did not reveal its methodology.

24   Friedrich Wu, Poa Tiong Siaw, Yeo Han Sia and Puah Kok Keong, 'Foreign Direct Investments to China and Southeast Asia: Has Asean Been Losing Out?', *Economic Survey of Singapore*, 2002.

25   Under International Monetary Fund guidelines, FDI is defined when an investor based in one country acquires an asset in another country with the intent to manage that asset (IMF, 1993, IMF and OECD, 2000). The IMF threshold is 10 per cent ownership of the ordinary shares or voting power or the equivalent for unincorporated enterprises. The IMF definition is adopted by most countries and also by the United Nations Council for Trade and Development (UNCTAD) for reporting FDI data in its annual publication entitled *World Investment Report*.

A Retrospective Survey: Comparing and Contrasting Sino-Indian Performance (Post-1980 Period)

4

A striking aspect is that both China and India gradually abandoned their earlier autarkic economic philosophy for a more outward-looking model, though more aggressively pursued by the former. Prior to the onset of reforms, both had sought to emulate the Soviet strategy, with a focus on heavy industries via their famous Five Year Plans.[1] Both employed a strong centralized approach to developmental strategies and resource mobilization through macroeconomic management (i.e., nationalized banks, control over trade) and microeconomic management (i.e., price controls, business licenses).

The general underlying motivations for changing course were similar as well. Both sought a dramatic change in economic direction, as previous strategies produced inadequate results—a market-oriented approach—the 1978 Deng Reforms and 1991 Rao Reforms. It may be noted that neither country had a seamless policy evolution. The 'stop-go' cycle in Deng's Reforms till 1989 is similar to an observation on Indian reforms, which, it has been argued, has been in five-year spurts of radicalism followed by a quiescence when it again flares up under political and economic pressures.[2] However, while Deng's control over Chinese reforms became near absolute by the early 1990s, India's democratic realities prevented the emergence of a sustained and enduring policy direction.[3]

At least, since the 1950s, following the detailed empirical work of Nobel Prize winner Simon Kuznets, the pattern of development has been understood to be in a sequence from agriculture to manufacturing to services. India, however, has grown rapidly (among the fastest in the world) without a robust manufacturing-sector growth. (The structural causes for this Indian 'puzzle' are discussed later). The biggest contributors to the change in the share of services in GDP were, in order; banking, wholesale and retail trade, community services, and communication. China, on the other hand, displays a more conventional path to development (see Chart 4.1, Chart 4.2 and Chart 4.3).

Kochhar et al point out that while India's share of services in overall GDP has increased from 37 to 49 per cent in the last two decades, the share of

Chart 4.1 Sectoral Contributions to GDP, 1980

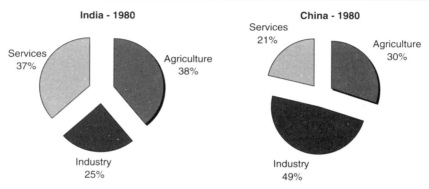

India - 1980

Services
37%

Agriculture
38%

Industry
25%

China - 1980

Services
21%

Agriculture
30%

Industry
49%

Source: Global Insight, Economist Intelligence Unit (EIU).

Chart 4.2 Sectoral Contributions to GDP, 2003

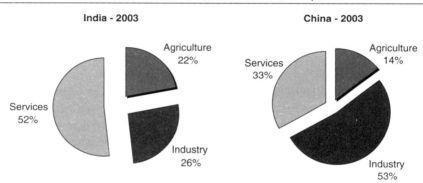

India - 2003

Agriculture
22%

Services
52%

Industry
26%

China - 2003

Services
33%

Agriculture
14%

Industry
53%

Source: India data from 'Checking India's Vital Signs', *Mckinsey Quarterly, 2005*; China data from *China Statistical Yearbook, 2005*.

Chart 4.3 Sectoral Contributions to GDP, 2006

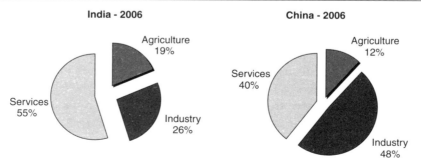

India - 2006

Agriculture
19%

Services
55%

Industry
26%

China - 2006

Agriculture
12%

Services
40%

Industry
48%

Source: India data from 'RBI Annual Report 2007'; China data from *China Economic Quarterly, 2007* Q2

manufacturing has remained more or less constant at 16 per cent. They also show that the change in the share of manufacturing during this period in India has been about 2.5 percentage points lower than the average country at the same stage of development, while the change in the services share was about 10 percentage points higher than average (even though its employment performance was below average). They write, 'In sum then, Indian manufacturing showed signs over the post-1980s period of not keeping up with the average performance in other similar countries'.[4]

It may also be noted that even though China's cross-border services trade (largely manufacturing-related services) represents a smaller proportion of its GDP relative to India, China's service sector in general is significantly more integrated with the global economy in terms of both cross-border trade and investment.[5]

In Chart 4.4, value-added share of China's service sector increased by 8.7 percentage points and its labour share rose by 5.3 per cent. India's service sector's share of GDP rose by 7 per cent, while its contribution to employment only increased by 2 per cent. Thus, employment elasticity of India's service sector is at roughly 0.3, much lower than China's figure of 1.64.

Chart 4.4   Service-sector Growth and Employment Generation

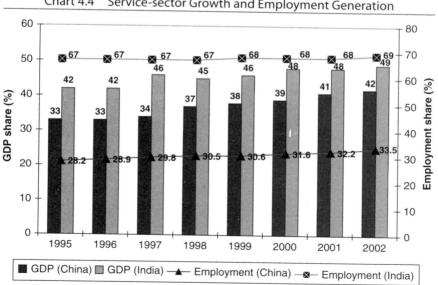

Source: Deunden Nikomborirak, 'A Comparative Study of the Role of the Service Sector in the Economic Development of China and India (Revised report)', Thailand Development Research Institute, 19 June 2006.

The inter-sectoral reallocation of labour supply created employment generation in China's service sector from both the manufacturing sector (after 1997) and the agricultural sector (pre-1997). The decline in employment against the rapid output growth in China's manufacturing sector also indicates productivity gains.[6] Chart 4.5(a) does not capture two important qualitative factors: (1) the reallocation of labour from the state-owned sector into the more dynamic industrial non-state sector in general since the early 1990s (2) increases in educational attainment of the labour force. It may also be noted that recent surveys suggest that one-third of manufacturing workers are in export-oriented sectors, which is equivalent to only 6 per cent to 7 per cent of the total workforce (750–800 million) or 50–60 million workers.[7] Chart 4.5(b) clearly shows the reallocation of the Chinese labour force away from the primary sector (agriculture) towards industry and services.

In India's case, the number of people employed in the organized sector, like agriculture, manufacturing, and services barely changed in a decade (see Chart 4.6). Moreover, the absence of a fall in employment in the agricultural sector is contradictory to the orthodox development experiences of transition economies. India's jobless service-sector growth stems from the fact that the

Chart 4.5(a)   Employment in China

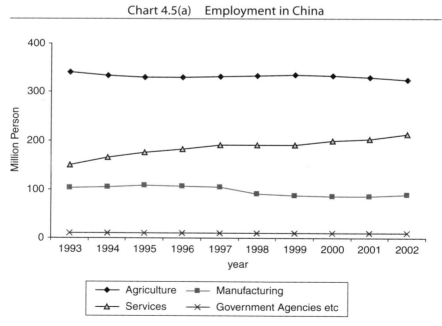

Source: *China Statistical Yearbook, 2004*

Chart 4.5(b) Changing Composition of Employment in China

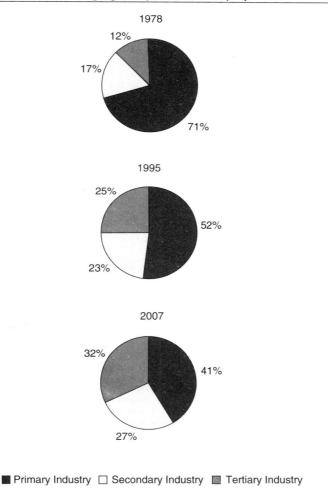

■ Primary Industry ☐ Secondary Industry ▨ Tertiary Industry

Source: *China Statistical Yearbook, 2008*

sector's growth has been driven largely by a handful of service sub-sectors—that is, banking, telecommunications, and IT-enabled services (ITES). Additional employment generated by these sectors was not able to offset the rapidly falling labour–demand elasticity faced by other service sub-sectors.[8] Further, given the skill-based model of these service sub-sectors, it is unlikely that labour-supply reallocation could occur from the unskilled rural supply, though the recent shortage of manpower in ITES and banking may have drawn its labour supply

Chart 4.6   Organized Employment in India

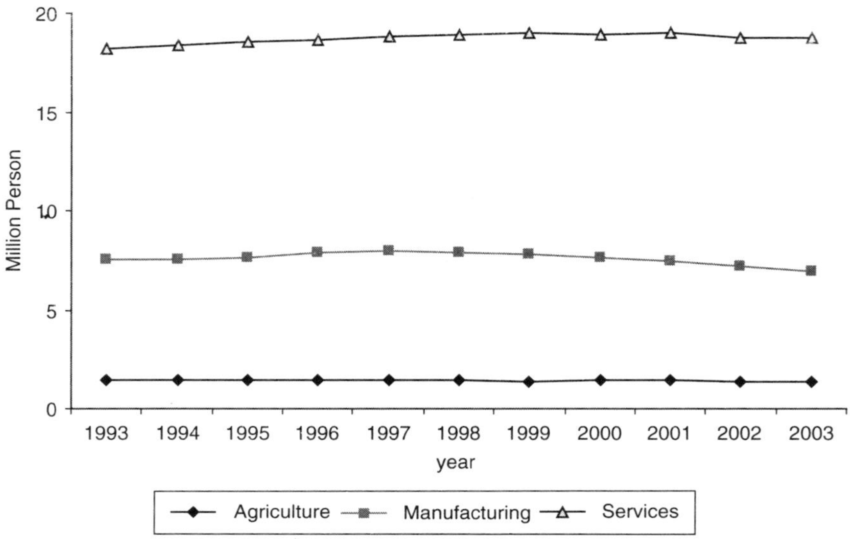

Source: Ministry of Finance, India; *Economic Survey, 2005–2006*

from the manufacturing sector. Importantly, in comparison to China, India is yet to achieve high levels of organized labour-force participation.[9] Ninety per cent of India's workforce is in the unorganized sector.

This is also manifested in the urbanization trend in China vis à vis India in Chart 4.7 below:

The pattern in Chart 4.8 clearly shows that China's growth has stemmed from its rapid integration into the world trading system. By the end of 2007, China had emerged as the world's second-largest exporter. FIEs account for 50 per cent of its exports. That the Chinese economy was FDI driven was a discernable feature even before its WTO entry in 2001. China now accounts for 55 per cent of Asian exports, 7.2 per cent of world imports, 16.5 per cent of global import growth, and an astounding 16 per cent of global GDP growth. All this is consistent with the now well-recognized trend of a reordering of Asian exports to Western markets via China, which has emerged as a central hub of transnational production value chains over the last decade.

China has two 'types' of exports—processed, finished, consumer, electronic products (with high-technology components that are imported) and unskilled-labour-intensive manufactures (furniture, toys, garments, shoes). Notice the diminishing share of unskilled-labour-intensive product

Chart 4.7 The Urbanization Trend in China vis-à-vis India

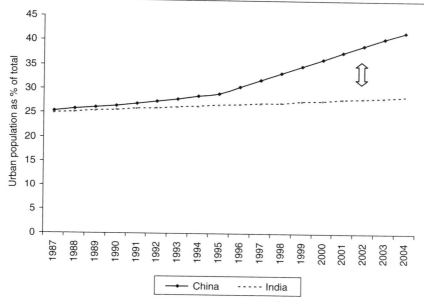

Source: Asian Development Bank, Key Indicators 2005

Chart 4.8 Trade: A Comparative Perspective

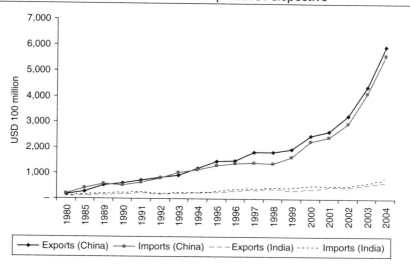

Source: China data from *China Statistical Yearbook, 2005*; India data from RBI

lines and the increasing share of capital- and technology-intensive processed exports (see Chart 4.9). However, it should also be noted that assembly activities within the production process in China (both component assembly and final assembly) are relatively low-technology and highly labour-intensive and, thus, less sophisticated than the manufacturing of the imported components themselves. Furthermore, MNCs have accounted for the majority of China's processing trade. From 1985 to 2007, foreign-invested enterprises (FIEs) exports and imports increased their share from 10 per cent to 60 per cent.[10] Seventeen of the top twenty FIE exporters are in electronic-related manufacturing. Chart 4.10 illustrates the types of exports and Chart 4.11 the exports by type of enterprises in 2004 with the help of pie diagrams.

India, on the other hand, has adopted a more gradualist approach to trade liberalization combined with a more indigenous service-oriented growth, which for the most part is characterized by its non-tradable feature.

Another striking aspect of the concurrent rise of both economies, endowed with a surplus labour force (1.2 billion), has been a global shock to labour-intensive industries (see Table 4.1). To the extent that India is yet to capture a significant share of global industrial labour-driven output, the

Chart 4.9   Types of Exports

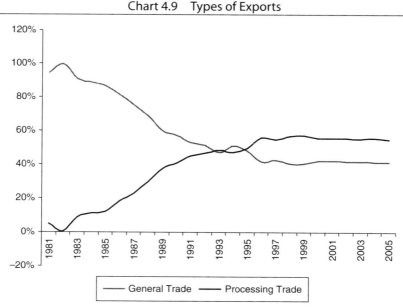

Source: *China Statistical Yearbook, 2006*

Chart 4.10 Types of Exports, 2004

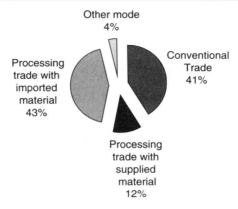

Source: Department of Planning and Finance, Ministry of Finance, 2005

Chart 4.11 Exports by Type of Enterprises, 2004

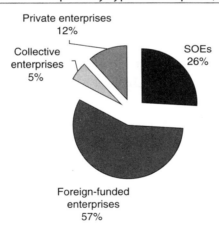

Source: Department of Planning and Finance, Ministry of Finance, 2005

Table 4.1 The Change Doubled Global Labour Force

	Millions of Economically Active Persons			
	Global	Advanced	LDC	New
1980	960	370	590	—
2000 Before	1,460	460	1,000	—
2000 After	2,930	460	1,000	1,470*

Source: tabulated from ILO, laborsta.ilo.org/
*China, 760; India, 440; Ex-Soviet, 260

implications are yet to be wholly discerned. Nonetheless, China's emergence as the central element in transnational production networks has adversely affected the competitiveness of OECD economies.

CONTRASTING SINO-INDIAN PERFORMANCE

Both China and India entered the 1980s at comparable levels of per capita income following three decades of growth—China at an average rate of 4.4 per cent per annum, and India at a rate of 3.75 per cent.[11] The subsequent divergence is captured in Chart 4.12 below:

In the 25 years after 1978, China's economic story surpassed India's as its per capita income trebled, while India's merely doubled. China's integration with the global economy too dwarfs India's external linkages. Angus Maddison has shown that by 1998, China had US$ 183 FDI per capita versus India's US$ 14 FDI per capita.[12] Indeed, by 2004, China had absorbed US$ 500 billion in cumulative FDI.[13] There is a wide consensus that compared to India, the Chinese were better 'socialists' during the planning era and better 'capitalists' during the reform era.

The Chinese economic story can be broadly categorized by the three waves of reform since 1978: (1) Reform of collective farming via the household responsibility system (2) Fiscal decentralization in the mid-1980s,

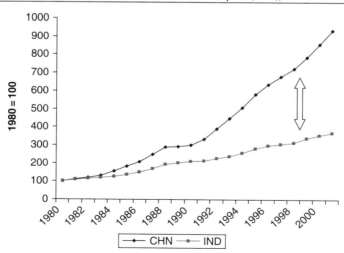

Chart 4.12   China and India: GDP Per Capita (PPP), 1980–2001

Source: *World Development Indicators*, World Bank

which led to the flourishing of township and village enterprises (TVEs) and reallocation of the labour force from agriculture to local industry (3) Deng Xiaoping's famous 'Southern tour' in September 1992 and the onset of radical reforms, which led to greater private-sector participation and FDI inflows.

Chinese reforms began with a focus on agriculture. After an analysis of the productivity of the non-agriculture sector in China, Alwyn Young, a professor at the University of Chicago, came to the following conclusion, which is consistent with much of the classical theory of economic development:

> Despite popular academic emphasis on industry and exports, a deeper understanding of the world's most rapidly growing economies may lie in the most fundamental of development topics: agriculture, land and peasant[14]

While land continued to be publicly owned, after the reforms, individual farmers had an incentive to produce more than their obligation, which they could dispose of in any way they chose. Thus post-reforms, Chinese peasants had the right to residual output after meeting their obligation to the plan[15]. This, along with an upward price adjustment for some agricultural products, provided incentives for households to use their underutilized labour resources intensively, which in turn, formed the source of demand for non-agricultural output.

Thus, while the rate of growth in agricultural output was 2.9 per cent from 1952 to 1978, it jumped to 7.6 per cent from 1978 to 1984. And this growth fuelled real per capita rural income growth to 15 per cent per year from 1978 to 1985. Given the thrifty rural sector, a significant proportion of savings was channelled into rural enterprises.[16]

Under the fiscal responsibility system introduced in 1984, local governments were increasingly accountable for economic development as financial assistance from the centre tapered off.[17] However, the local governments were free to develop local sources of tax and non-tax revenue. Such a hard budget constraint on local governments prompted them to vigorously promote TVEs (township and village enterprises), which not only met the growing rural demand for manufactures but also helped raise revenue for the local governments, which was used to build local infrastructure. The infrastructure then encouraged further investment. In aggregate, there was a reallocation, whereby the share of employment in agriculture fell from 62 to 53 per cent between 1978 and 1985, while the employment share in rural TVEs rose from 7 per cent to 14 per cent.[18] By the early 1990s, more than 120 million people had been transferred from agriculture to the TVEs.

Chart 4.13   Average Annual Growth Rate and Employment Share
of Agriculture, 1978–2003

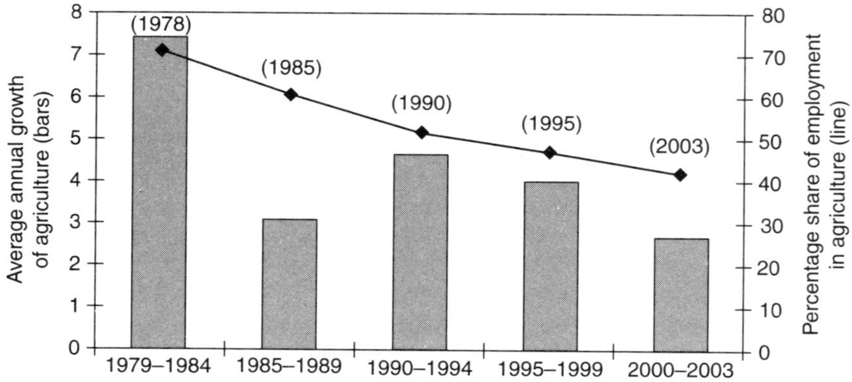

Source: Riedel et al, *How China Grows*, New Jersey: Princeton University Press, 2007, p. 6.

Subsequent structural transformation would continue, albeit at a slower rate, and by 2003, the share of employment in agriculture had dropped to 40 per cent (see Chart 4.13).

Nonetheless, by 1985, the growth effects of agricultural reform had been exhausted. Yet, China continued to post a 9 per cent plus GDP growth rate during the entire reform period. The reason was the growth of non-state owned TVEs (operating outside the central plan), which flourished in the 1980s after fiscal decentralization and the growth in domestic and foreign privately owned enterprises that drove industrial growth in the 1990s. It must be noted, however, that non-state-owned sector did not displace the state-owned sector, which continued to expand, albeit at lower rates (see Chart 4.14).

Along with the process of decentralization, China simultaneously sought to promote export of labour-intensive manufactures by developing infrastructure in the southern coastal cities. It encouraged foreign direct investment (FDI), especially from the non-resident Chinese from South-East Asia, particularly from Hong Kong to overcome the limitations of domestic entrepreneurship and technology to produce for the world market. China combined its cheap labour resources with Hong Kong's market-based institutions and business organizations to make a successful entry into world market for consumer goods.

This reorientation became necessary by the early 1990s as the SOEs' losses intensified and fiscal decentralization, as manifested by the rapid growth of

Chart 4.14   Industrial GDP in State-owned and Non-state-owned
Enterprises, 1980–2003 (RMB 100   illion)

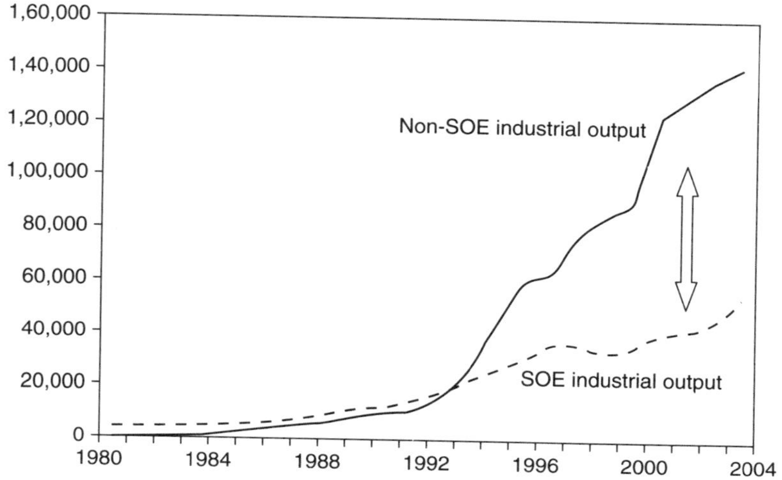

Source: Riedel at al, *How China Grows*, New Jersey: Princeton University Press, 2007, p. 10.

TVEs, was leading to the loss of macroeconomic control by the Central government. Growing socio-economic unrest at home exacerbated by seminal developments at the geo-political level (collapse of the Soviet Union), prompted the CCP to reassess the trajectory of subsequent reforms. It was in such a context that Deng Xiaoping's famous 'Southern tour' took place and in September 1992, the 14th Party Congress met in Beijing to mobilize support for radical reforms. In 1993, the CCP endorsed the concept of a 'socialist market economy' and began to formulate reforms that would replace the fiscal-contract system with a tax-assignment system that would be closer to fiscal federalism. The monetary system was recentralized and SOE reform gained currency. The private sector was acknowledged for the first time as a 'supplementary component of the economy' and upgraded to 'an important component of the economy' in September 1997, and finally incorporated in the Constitution in March 1999.[19]

Chart 4.15 shows the evolution of FDI flows. While in the 1980s, most FDI was in the form of joint ventures with SOEs, in the 1990s, most of it was wholly owned and in private joint ventures. Overall, the share of private firms in industrial output increased from an insignificant share in the mid-1980s to a majority 57 per cent in 2004.

Chart 4.15   Foreign Investment by Type of Ownership of Enterprise
Invested in 1988–2003 (RMB 100 Million)

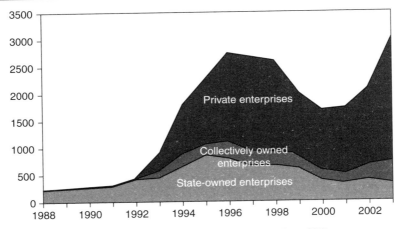

Source: Riedel et al, *How China Grows*, New Jersey: Princeton University Press, 2007

Zhang Jun, Professor of Economics and Director of the China Centre for Economics at Fudan University, has argued that China's growth has been driven by local governments induced to compete against one another, leading local governments and public–private alliances to build better infrastructure nationwide. Financial opportunities that became available to local governments were complimented by efforts such as allowing officials to travel and study abroad. These officials embraced FDI and marketization. In this manner, the political ideology of many individual leaders changed without fundamentally altering the structure of the political system as a whole. Professor Zhang notes that improvements in China's human capital have increased the legitimacy of its leaders and contributed directly to the flourishing of China's export industry.[20] Quite clearly then, China's growth has also been driven by a 'bottom-up' approach.

India's industrial growth turned around since 1980, after a prolonged period of relative stagnation during 1965–80. Export growth also picked up after the mid-1980s. However, there has been no acceleration in either the output or in export growth after the introduction of economic reforms since 1991, until very recently. In fact, industrial growth decelerated since the mid-1990s because of the slowdown in agricultural growth in the 1990s compared to the previous decade, and contraction in public-infrastructure investment for over one and half decades. After the mid-1980s, the pressure on public expenditure from rising deficits constrained public investment: from 1986 to 1987, public investment in GDP began a steady and deep decline from 11.2 per cent to 5.6 per cent of GDP in 2003–04.[21]

We alluded earlier to the 'Indian puzzle', whereby a massive agrarian economy coexists with a rapidly expanding service component (~50 per cent of GDP), while the manufacturing component lags behind. Structural constraints in India have created this pattern—a small pool of skilled workers (~25 million undergraduates or higher degree holders) and a simultaneous national illiteracy rate of almost 40 per cent. For instance, India spent 86 per cent of per capita GDP per student in tertiary education in 2000, while it spent 14 per cent of per capita GDP per student in primary education.

A legacy of an inefficient policy environment—the state unable to expand 'core infrastructure' goods that form a pre-requisite for a robust industrial base and rigid labour laws—constrained the use of a surplus factor of production. Rughuram Rajan, former Chief Economist at the IMF, describes this path as 'constrained adaptation', where an inherently entrepreneurial class filled a vacuum created by structural constraints, and channelled resources toward these service industries (where the relatively superior tertiary education sector had created an available base of skilled labour) that relied relatively less on physical infrastructure.[22] Thus, India's service sector was responsible for over 60 per cent of its GDP growth in the 1990s. And the growth acceleration was the strongest in business services, communication, and banking services, followed by hotels and restaurants, and community services. These five sub-sectors together accounted for the entire acceleration in services growth in the 1990s.[23] Thus, as an economist recently remarked, India's success in services has come, *in spite* of the government, rather than *because* of it.[24]

Devashish Mitra[25] also found that the rigid labour market, due to state labour rules and regulations and lack of infrastructure development, are the two fundamental factors stifling labour-productivity improvements, employment, and capital accumulation that would otherwise spur progress in India's manufacturing sector.

Importantly, India's reforms, unlike China's, never seriously addressed the agricultural (land reform) sector. While India's agricultural sector has lagged and is projected to grow at 2.5 per cent in 2007, China's has been consistently growing at 4 per cent to 5 per cent for the last 15 years. A few comparative statistics will be instructive.

According to the Food and Agricultural Organization (FAO), the average yield of rice in India between 2003 and 2005 was 3,034 kilograms per hectare (kg/ha). In contrast, the figure for China was more than double at 6,233 kg/ha. Similarly, for wheat, the corresponding figures were 2,688 kg/ha for India compared to 4,155 kg/ha for China. According to the International Rice Research Institute, India produced 124 million tonnes of rice compared to China's 186 million tonnes in 2004, despite having almost twice the area under paddy cultivation (42 million hectares versus 28 million hectares). In the profitable horticultural sector, while both India and China produced comparable 55 million tonnes and 60 million tonnes in 1980 respectively, by 2003, China had expanded to 450 million tonnes surpassing India's corresponding 135 million tonnes.[26]

According to Professor Huang Jikun, Director of the Centre for Chinese Agricultural Policy, the reasons for China having outperformed India in agriculture are threefold: technological improvements accruing from research and development; investment in rural infrastructure, specifically roads, storage, and marketing facilities; and an increasingly liberalized agricultural policy.[27]

Both countries have high saving rates (China—40 per cent versus India—28 per cent). So theoretically, neither faces capital shortage (saving–investment link), although, China is clearly more capital rich than India, and thus is able to generate huge internal savings to enable the state to focus on multiple socio-economic objectives[28]. Yet, China's rise has been based on a structurally fragmented economy—the SOEs have dominated the banking system (i.e., national savings) and hence, local capital was unable to be efficiently reallocated to private-sector development. This vacuum created an enormous demand and surge in FDI that the Chinese economy has readily absorbed over the last decade. Nonetheless, an enabling policy environment and state intentions toward creating an export-led growth were key factors in drawing FDI. The FDI that came in also had an incentive to create a 'parallel' infrastructure in the emerging coastal regions of the east. Yasheng Huang at MIT has documented this fragmented characteristic of China's growth.[29]

In comparison, India's, economy is more integrated with the implication that the PSUs, the providers of key public infrastructure 'goods', are intrinsically linked to the post-1991 liberalized private sector. Therefore, any PSU inefficiencies or inadequacies seep into the performance of India's private-sector industrial activity. Inefficiencies in the power sector alone have demonstrated this adverse effect on industrialization.[30] Since the export-driven model was not promoted as aggressively as China, and inferior governance and policy environment (i.e., effective SEZs, labour reforms) were lacking, India was unable to receive the FDI to spur its manufacturing-sector growth.

So China, which has amongst the highest savings rates in the world[31], still drew in huge foreign capital because indigenous savings were prevented from being channelled efficiently. Empirically, this seems to hold as during the

Chart 4.16   FDI as Per Cent of Gross Fixed Capital Formation (GFCF)

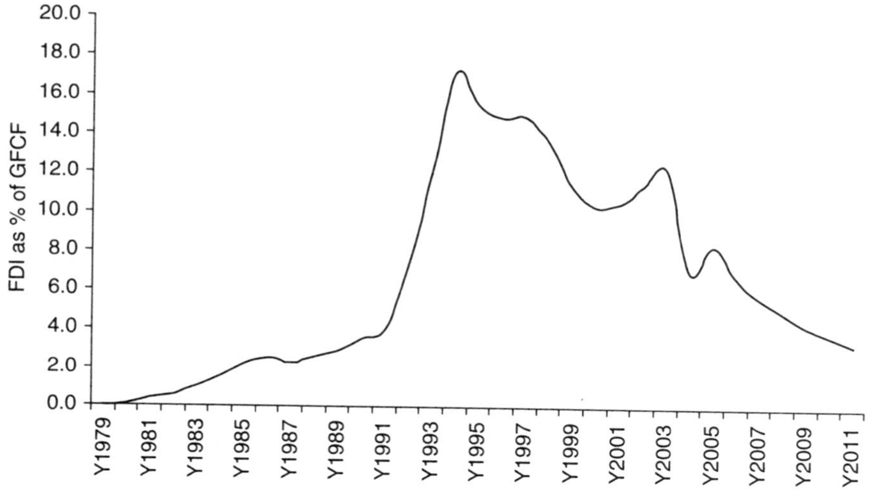

Source: *World Investment Report, 2004*, UNCTAD; Data for 2004–2011 from Economist Intelligence Unit (*World Investment Prospects to 2001*)

pre-1997 period, FDI increased, while domestic investing was constrained leading to a rising FDI/GFCF ratio (see Chart 4.16).

A second difference is the structure of the Chinese economy, which is essentially one of a decentralized nature. Each region is operationally and financially autonomous. Such an arrangement has led to the 'miniaturization' of Chinese firms, which cannot leverage on scale economies by operating in the larger Chinese economy. This fragmentation has segmented the markets for goods, services, and factors of production, which are not easily mobile across regions. Few Chinese firms develop alliances with or invest in companies in other provinces. For instance, one recent survey of 800 companies that have conducted domestic mergers and acquisitions found that 86 per cent of them invested in firms within their own city, 91 per cent within their own province.[32]

This immobility, especially of domestic capital has attracted foreign capital particularly in the remote interior regions of China, where domestic companies were restricted from investing. This was largely the consequence of fiscal decentralization, which created revenue incentives that encouraged provinces to engage in protectionist behaviour and practice 'backward specialization' by duplicating small enterprises across sub-national government jurisdictions. In effect, the centrally planned economy gave way to many regionally planned economies under provisional control.[33]

Interestingly, the contrast between the two economies implies that China's dual system (i.e., SOEs versus FDI-driven export sectors) meant that inefficiencies from the SOEs were insulated and contained, since the export-driven sector had its own captive infrastructure and policy-enabling environment. Indeed, until China's WTO entry, China ran a dualistic trade regime, with a relatively closed and protected domestic market and a relatively liberal export-promotion regime.[34] Dual foreign-exchange markets survived as late as 1994 and even dual real-estate markets (one for foreigners and one for locals) were maintained until as late as 2002.

In India's case, its 'integrated' economy, which theoretically ought to be an advantage, is currently characterized by public sector (i.e., 'core physical infrastructure'[35]) inefficiencies that drag down the manufacturing sector. Of course, the services sector in general and the information technology/software sectors in particular, which are relatively less capital-intensive and less reliant on core 'public goods' have unsurprisingly flourished, as have certain manufacturing sectors that have created their own captive sources of private infrastructure. In the final analysis, India's short-term disadvantage can perhaps be transformed into a longer-term advantage, given its 'integrated economic structure' relative to China's fragmented structure, which has its own challenges to connect the regionally distinct parts of its economic structure.

ADDRESSING THE FAULT LINES

Sanjay Hansda, an economist at the Reserve Bank of India, conducted a detailed input–output analysis and suggested that linkages from services to industry were strong.[36] An ICRIER (Indian Council for Research on International Economic Relations) working paper estimated manufacturing production functions for data from 1980–81 to 1997–98, and found that services inputs made a significant contribution to manufacturing output.[37] While neither of these studies posits a growth mechanism, they do support the intuition that services growth and innovation can spill over positively to manufacturing, just as China's national-accounts revision accords with the idea that its manufacturing prowess has also fuelled domestic-services growth. In fact, linkages work both ways: automobiles need servicing, while call centres need computers.[38] Indeed, a comparative study on the service-sector contribution to the overall growth in India and China notes, 'the fact that India may finally enter a manufacturing-sector boom will be a definite boon to the country's service sector, whose growth has been partially constrained by the absence of a parallel growth in the industrial sector'.[39]

The prospects for future growth will explicitly depend on further deepening and widening of reforms with both economies seeking a more diversified and balanced growth strategy. Until now, Chinese growth has been fuelled by its export-driven manufacturing industries. These have traditionally been concentrated in the eastern coastal parts of China. But with the adoption of a nationwide template, such industries are gradually relocating to the central and western provinces of China. The advanced eastern parts will then tend to attract higher value-adding industries, especially knowledge-driven ones, in the services sector. It is, therefore, imperative that China establishes a more robust IPR regime that would protect investors' rights. Moreover, the world is yet to fully witness the domestic-demand strength of China. The emerging middle class, 300–400 million, with rising per capita incomes will lead to a more domestic-driven economy.

Economic managers of both economies, however, will need to address specific 'fault lines' in their political economy to ensure further development.

In China's case, establishing institutions will be the next challenge. This is intrinsically linked to its dilapidated legal framework. China would need to develop a legal system that respects patent rights in a sound IPR regime to attract much-needed investment in research and development (R&D) and technology transfers. It would also need to restructure the banking and financial sector. These would have two consequences—(1) allow for more instruments and efficiency in macroeconomic management—fiscal and monetary policy, and, (2) China has enough capital—but it has done a bad job of efficiently allocating these savings to domestic industries. Finally, the important objective of China is to integrate the national economy by 'promoting beneficial interactions among the eastern, central, and western regions' in the 11th Five Year Plan (2006–11). With a rapidly expanding trade surpluses (over 9 per cent of GDP for 2007), Beijing has signalled its intention to rebalance growth by focusing on domestic demand. As part of the rebalancing agenda, the State Council released a document in March 2007 with guidelines to stimulate China's service-sector share of GDP by 3 per cent, by 2010.

In India's case, the central challenge would be to capitalize on its advantageous institutional, efficient property-rights market system and sound macroeconomic management, by expanding the supply of core infrastructure goods and services. In addition, a reformed, flexible labour regime would significantly enhance the prospects of a mass job-creating growth, and finally allow a take-off in large-scale manufacturing. In sum, India would need to successfully execute the second generation of industrial reforms, while significantly improving the prospects of its agricultural sector.

Both China and India would need to establish efficient and independent regulatory regimes. The current trend toward a private market-based model will require anti-trust regulators for different industries[40] (see Appendix for a policy note on India and anti-trust). Until now, given the predominance of SOEs/PSUs, there was little need for regulation as most industries were government-owned. Another common policy dilemma is HRD. Human resource development will be essential for China to graduate to higher-value-adding industries and for India to train a potentially enormous underemployed labour force. Enabling public and private spending on education is a major issue for both, though more critical for India. The second major shock to the 'global' labour market will occur when India's vast youth population—over 340 million under 17, compared to China's 240 million—enters industry over the next three decades. Translating this demographic dividend into sustained economic growth would require actively addressing the second generation of economic reforms in India.

To conclude, while the prospects for growth remain high, each economy, given their respective structural characteristics, face independent challenges to re-steer economic trajectory toward a balanced path.

NOTES

1   Note the similarity of planning institutions—China's State Planning Commission (1953) versus India's Planning Commission (Ministry of Finance).

2   Vijay Joshi, I. M. D. Little, *India's Economic Reforms, 1991–2001*, New York: Oxford University Press, 1996.

3   Meghnad Desai, 'India and China: An Essay in Comparative Political Economy', Paper for IMF conference on India/China, New Delhi, November 2003.

4   K. Kochhar, Kumar U., Rajan R., Subramanian A., and Tokatlidis I., 'India's Pattern of Development: What Happened, What Follows', IMF Working Papers, 2005.

5   Deunden Nikomborirak, 'A Comparative Study of the Role of the Service Sector in the Economic Development of China and India (Revised report)', Thailand Development Research Institute, 19 June 2006.

6   Ibid.

7   'Economics Focus, "An Old Chinese Myth"', *The Economist*, 3 January 2008.

8   Ibid.

9   This has largely been attributed to structural constraints—inflexible labour laws, low penetration levels of primary and secondary education.

10   Source: National Bureau of Statistics, China.

11   T. N. Srinivasan, 'China and India: Growth and Poverty, 1980–2000', Standford Center for International Development, Working Paper No. 182. September, 2003.

12   Angus Maddison, *The World Economy: A Millennial Perspective*, Paris: OECD Development Centre Studies, 2001.

13   It is worthwhile noting that FDI never accounted for more than 15 per cent of total investment in China. Given the large public sector in China's economy, it could be useful to isolate private-sector investment. The FDI/capital formation ratio net of investments by the public sector reveals China's high FDI dependency. By this measure, for the period 1992–1998, China's FDI/capital formation ratio was 27.9 per cent. FDI's importance has subsequently declined.

14   Alwyn Young, 'Gold into Base Metals: Productivity Growth in the People's Republic of China During the Reform Period', NBER Working Paper No. 7856, New Delhi, August 2000.

15   R. Nagaraj, 'Industrial Growth in China and India: A Preliminary Comparison', *Economic and Political Weekly*, 21 May 2005.

16   James Riedel, Jing Jin, and Jian Gao, *How China Grows: Investment, Finance, and Reform*, New Jersey: Princeton University Press, 2007, p. 5.

17   Prior to 1979, China's budgetary policy essentially consisted in generalized tax collection and profit remittances controlled by the Central government and then redistributed as needed to the provinces. This system of 'eating from one pot' was changed in the 1980 intergovernmental reform, under which, different jurisdictions were assigned different expenditure responsibilities and were also made responsible for collecting necessary revenues.

18   Ibid.

19   Ibid, pp. 12–13.

20   'China and the Future of the World', 28–29 April 2006, 'China's Future in the Age of Globalization', 29 April, Panel Discussion, http://chicagosociety.uchicago.edu/china.

21   T. N. Srinivasan, 'Comments on From "Hindu Growth" to Productivity Surge: The Mystery of the Indian Growth Transition', IMF Staff Papers, Vol. 52, No. 2, September 2005.

22   'India's Pattern of Development: What Happened, What Follows?', IMF Working Paper, January 2006.

23   Gordon, James, and Poonam Gupta, 'Understanding India's Services Revolution', IMF Working Paper WP/04/171, September 2004.

24   Nirvikar Singh (2006) has pointed out that telecommunications reforms did contribute to the rapid growth in IT and ITES sectors.

25   Devashish Mitra, *India Manufacturing: A Slow Sector In a Rapidly Growing Economy*, New York: Department of Economics, The Maxwell School of Citizenship and Public Affairs, Syracuse University, 2006.

26   Pallavi Aiyar, 'Agriculture: Where India and China Stand', *The Hindu*, 3 September 2007.

27   Ibid.

28   According to *McKinsey Quarterly*, 22 January 2006, India's financial stock in 2003 totalled 137 per cent of GDP compared with China's 323 per cent of GDP.

29   Yasheng Huang, *Selling China: Foreign Direct Investment During the Reform Era*, New York: Cambridge University Press, 2003.

30   Nirvikar Singh, at the University of California, in a recent analysis of input-output structure, identified 10 leading sectors in the Indian economy based on growth impacts on GDP of efficiency improvements in these sectors. These sectors include—electricity, water/gas supply, transport services, railway transport services, coal and lignite etc. He found that India's growth rate is at least as sensitive to these sectors as it was prior to the 1991 reforms. See Nirvikar Singh, 'The Ten Sectors that Need a Boost', *Financial Express*, 12 December 2006.

31   Between 1986 and 1992, the Chinese savings rate was 36 per cent, and between 1994 and 1997, it rose to 42 per cent. It currently is estimated in the mid-40s. (State Statistical Bureau).

32   Jinghai Zheng, Arne Bigsten and Angang Hu, 'Can China's Growth be Sustained? A Productivity Perspective', For the Special Issue on Law, Finance, and Economic Growth in China, *World Development*, 2007.

33   James Riedel, Jing Jin, and Jian Gao, *How China Grows: Investment, Finance, and Reform*, New Jersey: Princeton University Press, 2007, p. 12.

34   Barry Naughton, 'China's Trade Regime at the End of the 1990s: Achievements, Limitations, and Impact on the United States', in Ted G. Carpenter and James A. Dorn (eds.), *China's Future: Constructive Partner or Emerging Threat?*, Washington, D.C.: CATO Institute, 2000.

35   Broadly defined as generation and distribution of power, roads, bridges, rail systems, water supply projects, water treatment systems, irrigation projects, sanitation and sewerage systems or solid waste management system, ports, airports, inland waterways or inland ports.

36   Sanjay K. Hansda, 'Sustainability of Services-led Growth: An Input-Output Analysis of Indian Economy', RBI Occasional Working Paper, Vol. 22, No. 1, 2 and 3, New Delhi, 2001.

37   Rashmi Banga and B. N. Goldar, 'Contribution of Services to Output Growth Productivity in Indian Manufacturing: Pre and Post Reform', ICRIER Working Paper No. 139, New Delhi, 2004.

38   Quoted in Nirvikar Singh, 'The Services-Manufacturing Debate', *Financial Express*, 26 January 2006.

39   Deunden Nikomborirak, 'A Comparative Study of the Role of the Service Sector in the Economic Development of China and India (Revised report)', 19 June 2006, Thailand Development Research Institute. Also see Nirvikar Singh, 'Services-led Industrialization in India: Prospects and Challenges', Working Paper No. 290, Stanford Centre for International Development, Stanford University, August 2006, updated November 2006.

40   Recent indications suggest both governments are proposing to extend their oversight in this crucial public policy issue: 'India Plans New Panel to Look into Corporate M&As', *Reuters*, 29 August 2007; 'China Passes Antitrust Law, to Scrutinize More Deals', www.bloomberg.com, 30 August 2007.

China as a Manufacturing 'Hub': Intra–East Asian Geo-Economic Dynamics

5

It is now well-recognized that one of the most striking consequences of inward-manufacturing FDI has been the emergence of China as an integral link in global production value chains.[1] Thus, FDI and trade are intertwined in China's economic story. According to a recent report, 'World Investment Prospects to 2011', China's FDI inflows are projected at US$ 87bn per year for 2007–11. China is expected to rank third globally, behind the USA and the UK. China's projected share of global FDI inflows of 6 per cent in 2007–11 would be equal to its share in 2002–06.[2] It is also worth noting that 'vertical-intra-industry-trade- (VIIT) oriented FDI' in East Asia (including China) has been attracted to locations with inexpensive labour, clusters of enterprises capable of flexible production and timely delivery with few or no defects, access to infrastructure such as efficient ports, and policies that make it inexpensive to import intermediate goods (like duty-drawback schemes).[3]

Today 'production fragmentation' has become the dominant economic theme across East Asia. Production sharing with advanced Asian econo-mies has permitted rapid diversification in China's manufacturing exports. Firms in Asia have moved production facilities to China, enhancing China's integration in the regional economy and leading to the reorganization of industry in East Asia. And while China has emerged as the most impor-tant final assembly hub, Japan and the NIEs (newly industrialized econo-mies: South Korea, Singapore, and Taiwan) are, by far, the most important sources of innovative inputs into processing. Over the past decade, the proportion of components in exports to China has increased by almost 5 times for Indonesia, 15 times for Thailand, 19 times for Malaysia, and 60 times for the Philippines.[4]

In aggregate, such a vertical division of labour—the splitting up of the value-added chains between different East Asian countries, each specializing in a particular stage of the production sequence—has re-altered international economic dynamics. For China, participation in this division of labour has also been an important channel of technology transfer and helped China enhance the high-tech component of its exports.[5] Importantly, the construction of 'extreme interdependence' in East Asia has largely been a positive-sum game, contrary to the popular belief that China's economic juggernaut has crowded out opportunities for other emerging economies.[6]

FDI has also been integral to this process. Firms from the most industrialized economies—Japan, South Korea, Taiwan, Hong Kong, Singapore—have through FDI, initially outsourced their low-technology, labour-intensive export platforms to China followed by more 'know-how' FDI, as China moved up the outsourcing value chain. Intel Corporation's recent decision to set up a US$ 2.5 billion silicon-wafer fabrication plant in China, its first in Asia, is a sign of China's attraction as a 'high-technology' investment destination.[7]

For instance, nearly three-quarters of China's computer-related products are produced by Taiwanese companies, which are themselves dependent on OEM contracts with Japanese and US companies.[8] Such export-oriented FDI, driven partly by efficiency-seeking transnational companies and, partly by China's inherent comparative advantages in labour-intensive sectors, has led China to become the 'world's outsourcer of first resort'.[9] Taiwanese firms alone are responsible for 60 per cent of China's total information-technology exports.

Japan has set up more than 30,000 enterprises and joint ventures in China, with an accumulated investment of US$ 58 billion.[10] Similarly, South Korea had also set up more than 30,000 enterprises in China by the end of 2006, with an accumulated investment of US$ 35 billion.[11] Singapore has invested US$ 31 billion in over 16,000 projects in China.[12] While FDI data reports that Taiwanese companies have invested US$ 40 billion in mainland ventures, many believe the figure stands at a cumulative US$ 100 billion over the past decade.[13] More over, this relocation is not confined to downstream-assembly operations but has moved to mid- and upstream-components production.

Moreover, the structural interdependence is now getting more sophisticated. In this more complex network, Japan and the NIEs provide high-quality materials, including design, to their FDI affiliates in China and developing East Asia, which uses them to produce components. The components are then sent back to the originators for further processing. The originators perform quality control, organize the components, and send them back to developing East Asia as kits for final assembly.[14]

Thus, production sharing in East Asia is largely a vertical, intra-industry-trade phenomenon in which transactions are characterized by back-and-forth trade links, whereby several countries in the region participate in various stages of single-production chains.[15] China has gradually moved away from being simply an assembler of components. Increasingly, mainland production is integrating backwards and the supply chain is moving to where the assembly is undertaken.[16]

Today, the G3 economies—The USA, EU, and Japan—the major export destinations of global exports, account for 43 per cent of Asia's total exports, down from 53 per cent two decades ago. The share of intra-regional trade in total exports rose from 26 per cent in 1985 to 37 per cent in 2005 (see Chart 5.1 and Chart 5.2).

Importantly, however, the structural feature of intra-Asian trade is the phenomenon of transnational supply chains, where the final destination of

---

Chart 5.1   Composition of Asian Exports, 1985

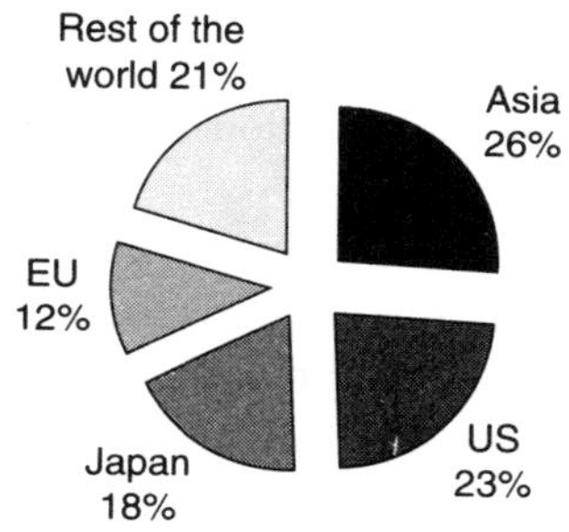

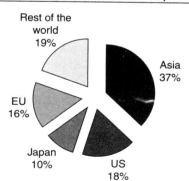

Rest of the world 21%
Asia 26%
EU 12%
Japan 18%
US 23%

Source: 'Direction of Trade Statistics CD', International Monetary Fund, January 2007.

Chart 5.2   Composition of Asian Exports, 2005

Rest of the world 19%
Asia 37%
EU 16%
Japan 10%
US 18%

Source: 'Direction of Trade Statistics CD', International Monetary Fund, January 2007.
Note: Asia comprises People's Republic of China; Hong Kong; Indonesia; Republic of Korea; Malaysia; Philippines; Singapore; and Thailand.

finished products is extra-regional. More than 70 per cent of intra-Asian trade consists of intermediate goods used in production, and of this, half is driven by final demand outside Asia. Consequently, about 61 per cent of total Asian exports (instead of 43 per cent of the total exports as shown in Chart 5.2 for 2005 (EU 16 per cent, Japan 10 per cent, the USA 18 per cent) is eventually consumed in the G3 countries.[17]

Within Asia, China is the largest driver of regional exports, but its final demand accounted for only 6.4 per cent of the total Asian trade, which was only half the contribution from Japan and slightly below a quarter of that from the USA.

Thus, the G3 economies are still the main ultimate export destinations for final goods leaving Asia, when taking into account the share of intermediate-goods trade, that is, for assembly and production within the region but that are eventually shipped out of the region. This is hardly surprising since the G3 economies still account for around 55 per cent of the global annual income. In aggregate, then, globalization rather than regionalization is the dominant theme.

Importantly, China is at the epicentre of this growing intra-firm and intra-industry trade as the region's primary production base.

In the 1980s, the share of Asian neighbours in China's total exports rose steadily, while that of G3 markets declined. However, since the 1990s, the share of G3 markets has started to increase in terms of total Chinese exports, reaching to over 50 per cent by 2005. Meanwhile, China continued to import more from the rest of Asia in the 1990s, even with the declining share of Asian neighbours in its total exports (see Chart 5.3).

The growth rates of Chinese exports to G3 have been highly correlated with those of Chinese imports from the rest of Asia since the late 1990s. The basic pattern of PRC trade can be characterized as increasing exports to the global economy, while importing more intermediate goods from the rest of Asia. This trend is particularly pronounced in the electronics and automobile industries. For example, 15.5 per cent of China's total exports consisted of machinery and transportation equipment in 1992. By 2005, this figure had risen to 46 per cent. In the same period, the share of machinery and transportation equipment in China's total non–oil imports increased from 39 per cent to 48 per cent.

Chart 5.4 nicely captures the economic interdependence that China has established both with East Asia and with the USA and EU.

Importantly, while the more advanced economies (Japan, South Korea, Taiwan, and Singapore) are losing trade share in third countries, they are

Chart 5.3   Shares in PRC Trade, 1981–2005

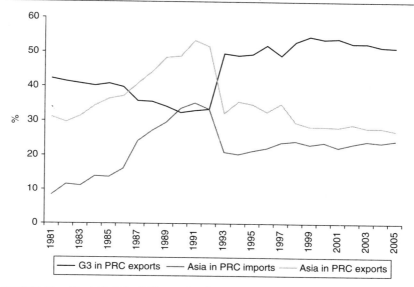

Source: 'Direction of Trade Statistics CD', International Monetary Fund, January 2007.
Note: Asia comprises People's Republic of China, Hong Kong, Indonesia, Republic of Korea, Malaysia,
Philippines, Singapore, and Thailand.

Chart 5.4   Correlation in PRC Trade

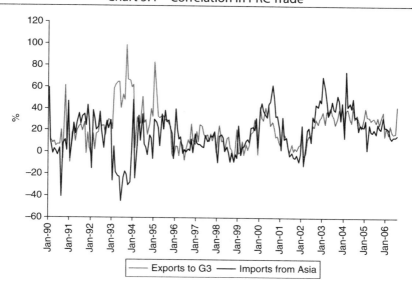

Source: 'Direction of Trade Statistics CD', International Monetary Fund, January 2007.

gaining in China. By early 2007, China had displaced the USA as Japan's top trade partner, with bilateral trade at US$ 207 billion (2006). China–South Korea trade was US$ 134 billion (2006). China–Singapore trade was US$ 41 billion (2006). China–Taiwan trade was US$ 80 billion (2006). Finally, China–ASEAN trade stood at US$ 190 billion (2007 projected).

The shares of Chinese imports of total manufacturing coming from East Asia increased from 64 per cent in 1992 to 76 per cent in 2004. This increase was dominated by components. The regional share of the total Chinese imports of components increased from 30 per cent to 78 per cent for the same period. Indeed, components accounted for over 90 per cent of the total increment in Chinese intra-regional manufacturing imports between 1992 and 2004 (see Chart 5.5). That such a division of labour has not been a zero-sum game is reflected in the remarkable export performance of East Asia; merchandise exports have increased by a factor of 13 since 1985, Chinese exports have surged by a factor of 20 (see Chart 5.6). Components production has clearly dominated East Asian manufacturing.

In general, FDI inflows to Asia have been closely linked with the establishment of regional production networks by MNCs. Recent research also

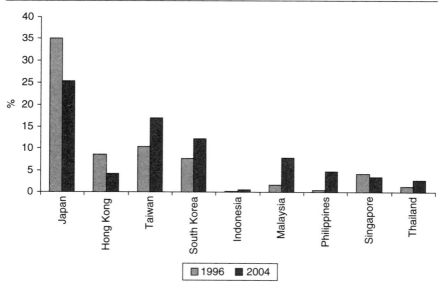

Chart 5.5   Country Share in China's Total Component Imports

Legend: ▨ 1996 ■ 2004

Source: Prema-Chandra Athukorala, 'Multinational Production Networks and the New Geo-Economic Division of Labour in the Pacific Rim', Departmental Working Papers from Australian National University, Economics RSPAS, 2006.

Chart 5.6   Share of Components in Total Manufacturing Exports

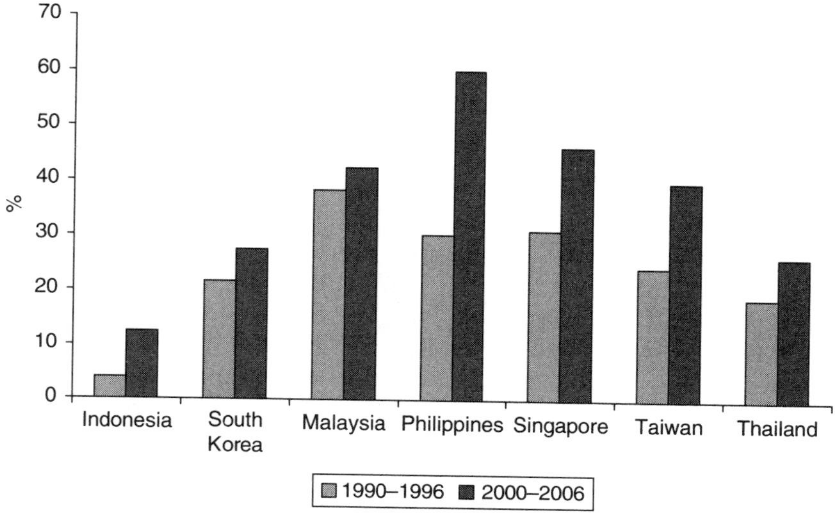

Source: 'Export Dynamics in East Asia' in *Asian Development Outlook, 2007 Update*, ADB

finds that rapid growth in FDI inflows to China have had positive spillovers to other Asian economies, as these form part of the same global production networks.[18] As China has expanded its role as Asia's primary production hub, this has also influenced the region's cross-border investment flows. Specifically, the share of FDI flows from regional economies to China has been noteworthy. East Asia (including Japan) accounted 50 per cent of FDI inflows in 2005 (see Chart 5.7).

ARE CHINA'S MANUFACTURING CAPABILITIES GROWING?

Clearly, OECD economies are still dominant in high-technology manufacturing and innovation. China accounted for about 8 per cent of worldwide value addition in manufacturing in 2002, making it the third-largest manufacturing economy in the world, behind Japan and the United States, but ahead of Germany (see Chart 5.8). However, when adjusted for the size of GDP (as China's GDP was a fraction of that of the USA, Japan and Germany in 2002), China has clearly demonstrated its manufacturing capabilities.

Chart 5.7   Source of FDI Inflows to PRC

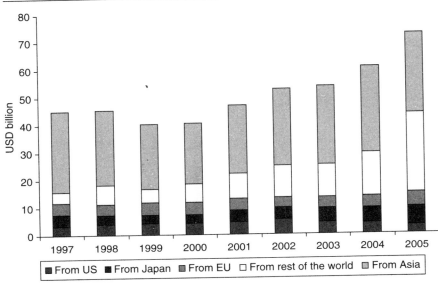

Sources: *China Statistical Yearbook*, various issues
Note: Asia comprises People's Republic of China, Hong Kong, Indonesia, Republic of Korea, Malaysia, Philippines, Singapore, Taipei, and Thailand.

Chart 5.8   Share of Major Regions in Global Manufacturing Value Added (Per Cent), 2002

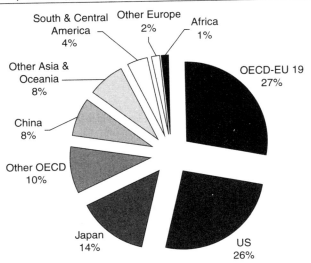

Source: OECD Science, Technology and Industry Scoreboard 2005, OECD, 2005, p. 179.

Chart 5.9   Contributions of Industries to Trade Balance as Per Cent of
             Manufacturing Trade by Technological Intensity, 2005

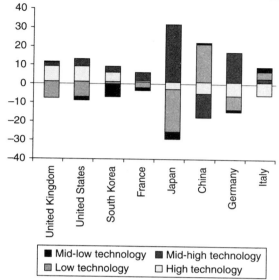

Source: OECD Reviews of Innovation Policy, China, Synthesis Report, OECD, 2007, p. 10.

Chart 5.9 clearly shows that China is still largely specialized in low-technology manufacturing. China's negative trade balance in mid- and high-tech products appears consistent with the general perception of Chinese participation being largely at the lower end of the manufacturing value chain. Overall, 65 per cent of Chinese exports are accounted by mid- to high-skill processed manufacturing. However, the composition of China's processing exports has evolved. China's share of assembling high-end technology components (i.e., semiconductors, microprocessors) and exporting finished products accounts for 50 per cent of processing exports (and ~35 per cent of total exports). Around 65 per cent of these exports are accounted for by wholly foreign-owned firms.

As of 2004, China is the world's largest exporter of ICT (information and communication technology) equipment (see Chart 5.10). In 2006, such electronic products accounted for 42 per cent of the total manufacturing exports.[19] Moreover, China's success is not simply a story of specialization according to comparative advantage. Its export bundle is that of a country at a level of per capita income three times higher than the country's actual level.[20] A caveat here should be noted in that FIEs account for the majority of mid-high technology exports out of China.

Chart 5.10   Exports of Information and Communication Technology Goods

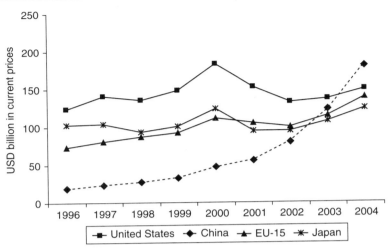

Source: OECD, International Trade Statistics database.

What this chapter seeks to illustrate is the high extent of Chinese integration with the East Asian economies, and its simultaneous emergence as the principal economic interface for the USA and the EU in Asia. We should, however, be cautious not to interpret these geo-economic trends by exaggerating Chinese economic power and industrial capabilities, since it is abundantly clear that China does not possess the autonomy, so far, and is heavily dependent on regional industrialized economies and massive investment by Western MNCs (led by the USA) to sustain its export juggernaut. The chapter's analysis also underscores the futility of employing bilateral trade and investment statistics as a measure for assessing Chinese trading success and the involvement of extra regional actors in the Chinese economy. As Shaun Breslin notes:

> It is not a case of the East Asian regional economy rising as a challenge to the US as some would suggest, but rather a case of US economic actors being inextricably interlinked with the regional economy itself ... China is acting as the manufacturing conduit through which the regional deficit is processed.[21]

Over the longer term, whether such asymmetric interdependence gradually evolves—as more advanced economies such as the USA and Japan move higher value and more high-technology manufacturing processes and R&D to mainland China—into autonomous Chinese industrial capabilities or simply subcontracted manufacturing enclaves for MNCs on the eastern seaboard remains unclear for now. Such a trend will be shaped more by the Chinese political economy and broader geopolitical variables than economic logic alone, and is beyond the scope of the present study.

NOTES

1   Gaulier, Lemoine and Kesenci, 'China's Emergence and the Reorganization of Trade Flows in Asia', CEPII, Working Paper, March 2006; Zheng, Wern and Tai You, 'China's Rise as a Manufacturing Powerhouse: Implications for Asia', MAS Staff Paper No. 42, Dec 2005; Haddad, Mona, 'Trade Integration in East Asia: The Role of China and Production Networks (1 March 2007)', World Bank Policy Research Working Paper No. 4160.

2   'Three Asian Giants', *The Economist*, 6 September 2007; 'World Investment Prospects to 2011: Foreign Direct Investment and the Challenge of Political Risk', Economist Intelligence Unit and Columbia Program on International Investment, 2007.

3   'The Drivers of Trade and Integration in Asia', *Asian Development Outlook 2006*, Asian Development Bank (www.adb.org), pp. 269–275.

4   Mona Haddad, 'Trade Integration in East Asia: The Role of China and Production Networks (1 March 2007)', World Bank Policy Research Working Paper No. 4160.

5   To be sure, up to now, the technological upgrading of China's trade has largely remained circumscribed to the production and export networks of foreign firms. This is likely to change as Chinese MNCs emerge in their own right.

6   Prema-Chandra Athukorala, 'The Rise of China and East Asian Export Performance: Is the Crowding-out Fear Warranted?', Working Paper No. 2007/10, Departmental Working Papers from Australian National University, Economics RSPAS, September 2007; Sjamsu Rahardja, 'Big Dragon, Little Dragons: China's Challenge to the Machinery Exports of Southeast Asia', Policy Research Working Paper 4297, The World Bank East Asia and Pacific Region Financial and Private Sector Unit, August 2007.

7   'Intel Breaks Ground in China for US$ 2.5 Billion Silicon Fabrication Plant', *International Herald Tribune*, 8 September 2007.

8   Katsuhiro Sasuga, *Micro Regionalism and Governance in East Asia*, London, New York: Routledge, 2004.

9   Stephen S. Roach, 'The Heavy Lifting of Chinese Rebalancing', Morgan Stanley, *Global Economic Forum*, March 2002.

10   'Wen Calls for Further Development of China–Japan Trade, Economic Ties', *Xinhua*, 12 April 2007.

11   'Chinese Premier Says China–S. Korea Trade Cooperation Brings about Tangible Benefits', *People's Daily Online*, 11 April 2007.

12   'China, Singapore Agree to Further Economic Cooperation', *Xinhua*, 11 July 2007.

13   'World Investment Prospects to 2011', *Economist Intelligence Unit, 2007.*

14   Mona Haddad, 'Trade Integration in East Asia: The Role of China and Production Networks',World Bank Policy Research Working Paper No. 4160, 1 March 2007.

15   Mitsuyo Ando and Fukinari Kimura, *The Formation of International Production and Distribution Networks in East Asia*, NBER Working Paper 10167, National Bureau of Economic Research, Cambridge, MA, 2003.

16   Dani Rodrik, *What's So Special About China's Exports?*, NBER Working Paper 11947, National Bureau of Economic Research, Cambridge, MA, 2006.

17   'Trade and Structural Change in East and Southeast Asia: Implications for Growth and Industrialization', *Asian Development Outlook 2007*, pp. 82–100.

18   Barry Eichengreen and Hui Tong, 'Is China's FDI Coming at the Expense of Other Countries?', NBER Working Papers 11335, National Bureau of Economic Research, Cambridge, MA, 2005.

19   'Economics Focus, "An Old Chinese Myth"', *The Economist*, 3 January 2008.

20   Dani Rodrik, *What's So Special about China's Exports?*, NBER Working Paper 11947, National Bureau of Economic Research, Cambridge, MA, 2006.
      Note: This is also true for India's software and ITES exports, which one would not normally associate with India's level of income. We alluded to the structural features that fed this export bias for India. But note that China's export bundle also includes unskilled-labour-intensive 'soft manufactures' (2005 share of total exports was around 35 per cent)—toys, shoes, textiles—that are in line with comparative advantage patterns. India, however, has been unable to exploit this potential segment of its export basket.

21   Shaun Breslin, *China and the Global Political Economy*, New York: Palgrave Macmillan, 2007, p. 129, 146.

Lessons from China:
A Strategic Economic Policy for India

6

The discourse over China's economic story has consistently challenged the sustainability of Chinese growth over the medium and long term and has even speculated on the potential disadvantages of 'over investment' or creation of surplus capacities in China. Recent research, however, has now shown that investment has, in fact, been the fundamental driver of Chinese growth and served as a vital channel for technology absorption, productivity growth, and structural change.[1] Real gross domestic investment over the entire period—1980–2004—averaged a steady 37 per cent of real GDP[2] (see Chart 6.1). Moreover, manufacturing, infrastructure, and real estate have been the drivers of fixed-asset investment in China[3]—the building blocks for any aspiring industrial power. For the period 2003–2007, real fixed asset investment has grown at an average rate of 21 per cent.[4] Moreover, on a per capita basis, China still lags behind the industrialized world. In 2004, China's capital stock per capita was US$ 4,164, a fraction of the figure for the USA (US$ 152,367) or Japan (US$ 158,352).[5] Thus, further capital deepening is ineluctable as China becomes a richer economy.

Contrary to a widely held belief, that the return to capital in China is low, driven down by an investment rate in excess of 40 per cent of GDP, a recent paper by three prominent Chinese economists concludes that this is not the case: the rate of return decreased in the 1990s, but is now stable, at a high 20 per cent. This evidence suggests that the aggregate return to capital in China does not appear to be significantly lower than the return to capital in the rest of the world.[6]

Another measure of the efficiency of investment is the incremental capital–output ratio (ICOR)—the investment needed to generate an additional unit of output, measured as annual gross investment divided by the annual increase in GDP. Here again, the assumption has been that China's high capital–output ratio implies an inefficient economy. However, recent research suggests China's ICOR is closer to 3.1 in recent years, after adjusting for replacement investment, as seen in Chart 6.2. China's

Chart 6.1   Investment/GDP Ratio, 1995–2005

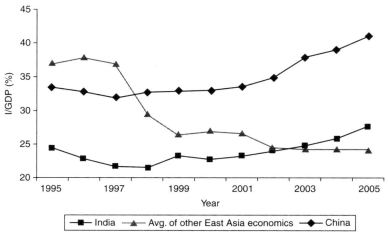

(Other East Asia Economies include Korea, Thailand, Singapore, Malaysia and Hong Kong)

Source: Shang-Jin Wei, 'Das (Wasted) Kapital: Is China Investing Too Much?', www.voxeu.org, 16 June 2007.

Chart 6.2   Incremental Capital Output Ratio (ICOR): Five-year Moving Average

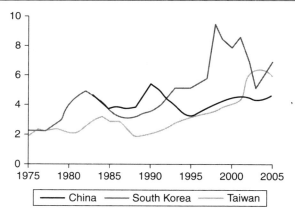

Source: ADB, Goldman Sachs

focus on infrastructure investment also explains the high ICOR. Infrastructure tends to undermine the return on investment in the short term, because the money is spent upfront, whereas the returns are spread over many years into the future, unlike manufacturing investment, where they appear sooner.[7]

Moreover, statistics on the high investment rates itself have also been overturned. A Goldman Sachs economist, Hong Liang, recently showed that the true investment rate is closer to 36 per cent–40 per cent, consistent with findings by Riedel, Andersen, at al that the investment boom is consistent with China's development stage, and sustainable, especially given the impending financial-sector reforms.[8]

Thus, that too much investment is creating a vast costly industrial overcapacity in China is simply exaggerated.[9] To the contrary, the ongoing trend of urbanization in China is likely to fuel further investment in infrastructure and housing-related sectors, in particular, electricity, water, and waste-treatment systems, as well as residential-property projects and non-tradable sectors in general. Chart 6.3 below shows the shares of fixed-asset investments made by China in 2006.

A recent comparative study on India and China has found that in comparable random samples of manufacturing businesses drawn from the two countries, Chinese firms are found to have higher total-factor productivity on the average than their Indian counterparts. First, the principal factor was that the average net-investment rate in fixed assets is higher in Chinese businesses. Second, the aggregate-productivity-growth rate was higher for the China sample because allocative efficiency gains are larger in Chinese industry. In China's case, reallocation of resources from the less efficient

Chart 6.3   Share (Per Cent) of Fixed-asset Investment (FAI), 2006

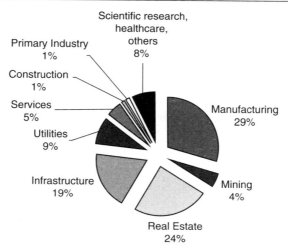

Source: Hong Liang, 'China's Investment Strength Is Sustainable', Global Economics Paper No: 146, Goldman Sachs, 3 October 2006

plants to more productive ones occurs faster.[10] Intuitively, this resonates in India's case, where structural constraints (i.e., labour inflexibility, access to capital) prevent efficient reallocation of resources (i.e., Indian firms are unable to rapidly liquidate failed investments).

In the earlier chapters, we elaborated on the export-oriented features of the Chinese economy, where FDI-driven export has fuelled the GDP growth. Of the top 500 companies, 280, accounting for 56 per cent, are from manufacturing industries, and less than 30 per cent are from the service-related industries. The industries are largely of the reprocessing type, where China has become a transnational assembly 'hub' or 'conduit' for other Asian exporters. Thus, the Chinese current-account surplus with the USA and EU also reflects an indirect surplus with other East Asian economies. In other words, the US trade deficit with China is, in fact, a de facto trade deficit with East Asia, which bilateral statistics do not and cannot capture. This aspect of China—as a massive trading economy—ensures China's external linkages in the global economy, and by creating powerful interdependencies, has arguably increased Chinese leverage in the international system. Tangentially, it may be also noted that such a complex multilateral chain also complicates attempts to impose costs on China's so-called 'mercantilist' policies, since protectionism against Chinese exports will inevitably punish other Asian economies that form an intrinsic (trade and investment) link in this transnational division of labour[11] (see Chapter 5).

Moreover, as China's exporters are penetrating new markets across the world and in Asia itself, the relative importance of different export markets is changing. For instance, in the first quarter of 2007, a slowdown of growth of exports to the USA and Japan was offset by a pick up in export growth to the EU, where by early 2007, China had surpassed the United States as the largest exporter to the EU.

Chart 6.4 suggests that Chinese export diversification has lowered its dependence on the US economy to sustain high export-growth rates. In the first ten months of 2007, Asia and the Middle East accounted for more than 40 per cent of China's export growth, North America for less than 10 per cent.[12] In 2006, the EU surpassed the USA as the largest importer from China. Today, China accounts for 8 per cent of world exports.

Simultaneously, China has also become a major driver for the global economy. In 2007, China is projected to surpass the USA's contribution to global GDP growth (16 per cent). In sum, China has become a second pillar, which is now supporting global growth (see Chart 6.5).

Chart 6.4   Share of Regions in China's Export (Per Cent)

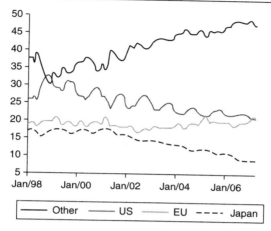

Source: *China Quarterly Update*, May 2007, World Bank

Chart 6.5   Contribution to Global Growth in Market Exchange Rates (Per Cent)

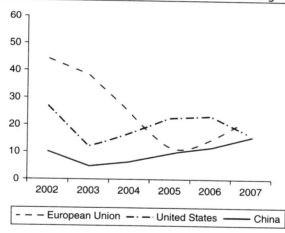

Source: *China Quarterly Update*, May 2007, World Bank

As Dani Rodrik notes, 'if China has welcomed foreign companies, it has always done so with the objective of fostering domestic capabilities.' Thus, in the consumer-electronics industry, China's specialty, '100 per cent foreign-owned firms are a rarity among the leading players in the industry. Most of the significant firms tend to be joint ventures between foreign firms and domestic (mostly state-owned) entities. A strong, domestic producer base has been important in diffusing imported technologies and in creating domestic supply chains'. Thus, 'government policies have helped nurture domestic capabilities in consumer electronics and other advanced areas that would most likely not have developed in their absence'.[13]

More recently, China is beginning to leverage its growing domestic market to draw in 'market-seeking' FDI, largely from the USA and EU. For instance, in the aviation sector, Beijing is employing its massive demand for civil aircraft[14] to induce MNC manufacturers to transfer production to China in lieu of securing long-term orders. In October 2006, Airbus agreed to open an assembly line for A320s with Chinese partners in Tianjin. Brazilian aircraft maker Embraer already produces jets in the northern Chinese city of Harbin, and made its first deliveries from the plant to China Southern Airlines in 2007. Such an external strategy for FDI, tied to market access, has coincided with an ambitious, indigenous programme by Beijing to develop a commercial, aircraft-manufacturing industry.[15] In 2008, China unveiled the Commercial Aircraft Corporation of China (CACC) in a drive to create a domestic civil-aviation-manufacturing sector. Premier Wen Jiabao noted that 'a review of international experience in aviation sector development shows that long-term and stable state support is a key factor in deciding the success or failure of large aircraft projects'.[16]

The Chinese model, then, has sought to achieve two parallel objectives— first, integrating with the international economic system largely through trade, and leveraging its huge comparative advantages (i.e., labour endowment, infrastructure) to attract further foreign investment and technology, thus expanding China's share in international supply chains. Such a pattern of backward integration in production implies that the supply chain is moving closer to the assembly hub—China. This suggests China has the potential to capture a greater value addition in the production cycle, as more sophisticated elements of the supply chains relocate to the mainland. Second, ensuring that during this process of integration, the Chinese state preserves its level of autonomy (and central control by the CCP) by counterbalancing external dependence and high economic decentralization as manifested by the success of TVEs, with a parallel state expansion in multiple heavy-industry sectors (via SOEs), occasionally with private-sector joint ventures.

It is worth highlighting that a key structural feature of the Chinese economy, in contrast to other transition economies, enabled this dual expansion of state and non-state sectors. Importantly, China (like India) began its reform process with most of its labour surplus in the rural sector (~80 per cent).[17] Thus, given this huge labour surplus, China could build a new and efficient labour-intensive, export-oriented, light industrial sector simultaneously with its pre-reform capital-intensive, state-owned sector.[18] In fact, such was the extent of labour surplus available, China was able to expand the state-owned sector (8 per cent per annum growth rate, 1978–1998) and construct a dynamic labour-intensive non-state sector, mainly comprised of the TVEs, whose share of industrial GDP grew from 22 per cent in 1978 to 78 per cent in 2001.[19]

This paradoxical strengthening of state and non-state/private sectors is arguably the fundamental feature of Chinese growth and also, the least analysed, especially from an economic-security perspective. In fact, China's use of SOEs and control over the financial sector to advance selective industrial policies is by no means a unique phenomenon. The evidence available from the East Asian and some European economies suggests they too employed SOEs as part of their development strategies.[20]

In aggregate, when Chinese growth is viewed from a comprehensive, national-security perspective, it appears that Beijing's policy planners have been equally concerned about China's economic autonomy, socio-economic and political stability and have, thus, calibrated its integration into the global economic system with a parallel drive toward robust state control over major portions of the national economy. And despite the reduced share of SOEs in industrial production and overall employment (see Chart 6.6), it is worth noting that SOEs still account for 35 per cent of total fixed-asset investment

Chart 6.6   SOE Output and Employment, 1985–2003

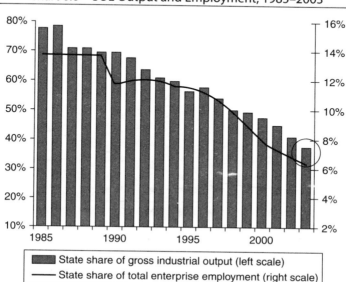

State share of gross industrial output (left scale)
—— State share of total enterprise employment (right scale)

Source: James Riedel, Jing Jin, and Jian Gao, *How China Grows: Investment, Finance, and Reform,* New Jersey, Princeton University Press, 2007, p. 9.

(though, down from the 65 per cent share in the early 1990s), 4 times higher than their share of total employment (8.5 per cent in 2004)[21] (see Chart 6.7 and Chart 6.8). Moreover, recent research suggests that any inefficiency in resource allocation in China caused by the SOEs or the banking sector have

Chart 6.7   Total Investment in Fixed Assets by Ownership, 2005

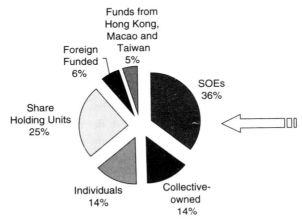

Source: *China Statistical Yearbook, 2006*

Chart 6.8   Total Investment in Fixed Assets by Ownership, 1995–2005

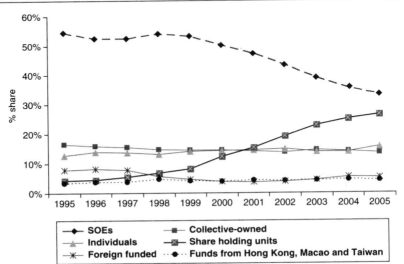

Source: *China Statistical Yearbook, 2006*
Note: Aside from SOEs and collective-owned, remaining are all private firms.

been outweighed by efficiency gains in the larger economy and at the corporate level.[22] The return on capital has increased for all type of enterprises in China. The return on equity for SOEs increased from 2 per cent in 1998 to 12.7 per cent in 2005, and 7.4 per cent to 16 per cent for non-SOEs.[23]

Since 1997, China has sped up internal reforms, particularly vis à vis domestic private companies. In 1997, the four largest state-owned banks were allowed to lend money to private companies. In 1999, for the first time, private domestic companies were also allowed to export directly. Thus, after 1997, when Beijing began the process of restructuring by allowing the SOE sector to reduce employment to improve profitability and allowed state-owned banks to lend to the private sector, the overall state sector has displayed improved margins. Today, the overall distribution of banking loans is shared almost equally between the state and private sectors (see Chart 6.9 and Chart 6.10). Consequently, SOEs financed over 50 per cent (2003) of their investment via internal accruals and informal finance. The even greater reduction of the share of collectively owned TVEs in total loans reveals the

Chart 6.9   Distribution of Loans by Ownership, 1988–1992

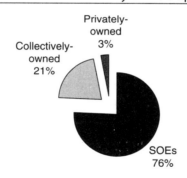

Source: *China Statistical Yearbook*, various issues

Chart 6.10   Distribution of Loans by Ownership, 2003

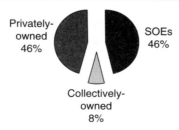

Source: *China Statistical Yearbook*, various issues

extent of decentralization of the economy since 1992. Collectively owned TVEs financed 73 per cent (2003) of their investment via internal accruals and informal finance.

Thus, it is clear that the state has shifted the burden of success for the collectively owned TVEs on their own efficiency and performance, which is consistent with the trend of decentralization of the Chinese economy since the mid-1980s. Since the late 1990s, Beijing's planners have also buttressed the status of private-sector participation in the overall macro economy. Yet, again it must be reiterated that the state sector has not been abandoned in this pattern of development.

PREPARING SOEs FOR GLOBALIZATION

Although China began SOE reforms in the 1980s, radical reforms only took place after Deng Xiaoping's 'Southern tour' in early 1992. In 1995, Zhu Rongji formulated a new strategy for SOE reform, which was called 'grasping the big and letting go the small'. It was officially adopted as a strategy in 1997. 'Grasping the big' meant making efforts to cultivate strong and competitive large enterprises and enterprise groups and develop them into cross-regional, cross-sectional, multi-ownership and multinational big firms. 'Letting go the small' implied that the government allowed the small and medium-sized SOEs to face market forces.[24]

In 1997, the Chinese government set a three-year phased goal to turn around SOE losses. While the objective of controlling SOE losses was largely achieved by the end of 2000, the implementation was criticized for not achieving substantial progress as the SOEs continued to face soft budget constraints. Moreover, 'grasping the big' concept had unintended consequences, as officials tried to use political and administrative means to merge enterprises in order to create giant monopolies, simply for the sake of 'big' and regardless of any other economic and social considerations. Thus, positive aspects of big enterprises, such as the capacity for innovation, efficiency and competitiveness did not develop as initially expected.[25]

In 2002, with the new Chinese government led by Hu Jintao and Wen Jiabao, the direction of SOE reform was further readjusted. In March 2003, China unveiled a new plan for reforming its SOEs—abandoning the earlier strategy of selling smaller state-owned firms and laying off workers to improve efficiency and productivity. Under the new plan, ownership of state compa-nies would be transferred from numerous ministries and commissions to a newly established central State-owned Assets Supervision and Administration

Commission (SASAC). SASAC was largely designed to resolve the principle-agent dilemma—separate the ownership and management aspects of SOEs, whereby firms are able to achieve greater autonomy in management (SASAC is a special organ of ministerial level directly under the State Council). Further, while responsibility was localized, which hitherto had been the mandate of many government departments that had administrative responsibility over enterprises, investors' rights were centralized from various departments. Since then, local SASACs have also been established in the provincial (autonomous region or municipality directly under the Central government) and municipal levels. As of end-2006, local SASACs supervised 1,031 SOEs.

Aside from being an investor, SASAC is also responsible for guiding the reform and restructuring of the SOEs, forming the board of supervisors in large SOEs on behalf of the state, human resource management, supervising and managing state-owned assets by statistical and audit means, and developing relevant regulations and laws. Managerial positions would be filled through open competition and no longer by administrative appointments. Thus, from 2003 to 2006, 81 senior posts in 78 central SOEs were openly advertised and recruited and 20 deputy senior posts in 10 central SOEs through internal competition.[26]

SASAC today oversees 161 central SOEs (down from 196 in 2003), which control the most powerful sectors of the economy. In December 2006, SASAC specified that seven sectors or 'life-lines of the national economy'—military equipment, electricity, oil and petrochemicals, telecommunications, coal, civil aviation, and shipping, must be either entirely controlled or dominated by state firms. SASAC noted that 'in these sectors, state-owned assets should expand in volume and optimize in structure, and some key enterprises should grow into leading world businesses'.[27] Presently, more than 40 of the 161 central SOEs are engaged in these sectors, with their total assets accounting for 75 per cent of all central SOEs, and 79 per cent of all profits.[28] In 2007, SASAC has undertaken stringent targets to induce greater autonomy and efficiency. SASAC will rate and rank the central state-owned enterprises (SOEs) based on a composite index, including profits, cost-control ability, core business profits, research and development expenditure, as well as rates of value maintenance and increment. Further, those central SOEs that fail to assume a leadership position (top three) in their respective industry groups will be compulsorily reshuffled by the government.[29] According to SASAC's plan, by 2010, the number of central SOEs should total 80–100, among which, 30–50 should be internationally competitive. This commitment to restructuring and merging inefficient SOEs is underscored by the fact that subsidies to loss-making SOEs have fallen over time and are now around US$ 2.5 billion (~two per cent of total SOE profits).

According to the National Bureau of Statistics, from 2003 to 2006, central SOEs saw their profits increase by 151.1 per cent from US$ 40 billion to US$ 100 billion for FY2006, of which almost 70 per cent was contributed by 9 large corporations.[30] The combined business revenue of China's top 500 companies accounted for 83.5 per cent of GDP in 2006. Of the total in the list, 349 enterprises or 70 per cent were state-owned or state-controlled.[31] Such a dual feature of the Chinese economy has provided it with a degree of autonomy and has at least partially insulated it from a potential slowdown in US markets, since Chinese macroeconomic managers would, when confronted with exports slowdown, be able to switch to domestic levers to raise aggregate demand.[32]

Further, insofar as all types of enterprises (state and private) in China largely finance their investment via 'self-financing' and domestic loans (see Chart 6.11 and Chart 6.12) rather than imported capital, the overall dependence of Chinese growth to international capital is almost non-existent (in fact, as American economist Lawrence Summers notes, 'the large flow of capital from the developing to the industrialized world has been the principal irony of the international financial system'[33].) And China has emerged as an important source of this 'global saving glut', which consequently sustains US macroeconomic over-absorption (current account deficits).[34]

Finally, note that surpluses from the Chinese exports as manifested by the enormous accumulation of foreign exchange reserves (see Chart 6.13)

Chart 6.11   Total Investment in Fixed Assets by Source of Funds, 2005

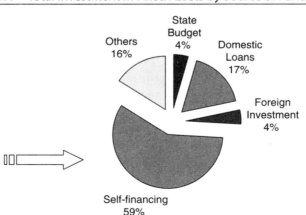

Source: *China Statistical Yearbook, 2006*

Chart 6.12   Total Investment in Fixed Assets by Source of Funds, 1981–2004

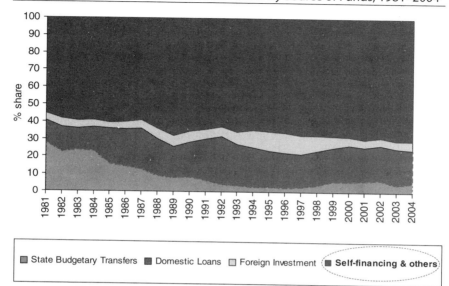

Source: *China Statistical Yearbook, 2005*

Chart 6.13   China's Foreign Exchange Reserves

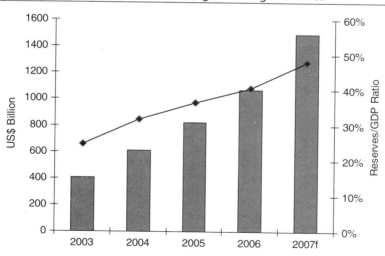

f = forecast
Source: *China Economic Quarterly,* 2007 Q2

growing at 35 per cent–40 per cent per year—US$ 1.9 trillion by December 2008, of which it recently stated that US$ 200 billion would be transferred into a Sovereign Wealth Fund (SWF), China Investment Corporation, and US$ 72 billion of which would be available for new investment[35]—have provided the state with command over a powerful economic instrument in its foreign relations; the ability to deploy capital in pursuit of geo-economic or geopolitical goals. In fact, this trend is in sync with a global pattern of state-backed investments, which are likely to emerge as an important variable in international financial markets and FDI flows in the coming decade. Already, according to the US investment bank Morgan Stanley, SWF assets are estimated at US$ 2.5 trillion, which is greater than assets under the global hedge fund industry. SWF assets are projected at US$ 5 trillion by 2010.[36]

China's Escalating Trade Surplus and 'Structural Rebalancing'

The 'self-financing' of investment has primarily stemmed from the rising profitability of Chinese enterprises since 2001 (see Chart 6.14). What is important to note here is the effect of top-line growth that is driving the volume of total profits, even as profit margins themselves have been fairly stable (5 per cent–6 per cent of sales). The sustainability of Chinese profit margins, in light of rising raw material and nominal-wage costs, stems from improved

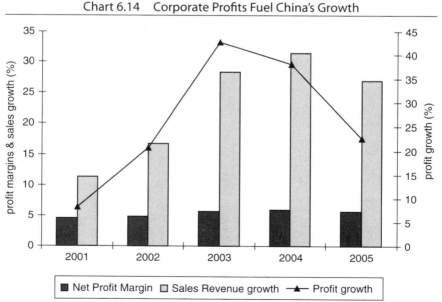

Chart 6.14   Corporate Profits Fuel China's Growth

Source: Bert Hofman and Louis Kuijs, 'Profits Drive China's Boom', *The Far Eastern Economic Review*, October 2006

technical efficiency and labour productivity (value-added per worker). The technical efficiency of the usage of intermediate inputs (in real terms) has improved substantially since 2003. It has been estimated that in most sectors in core manufacturing, the amount of intermediate input per unit of output (in real terms) declined 1.5 percentage points per year between 2002 and 2006. Similarly, for the overall manufacturing sector, while nominal wage costs increased at 14 per cent per year, nominal labour productivity grew faster at 21.3 per cent per year.[37] The ratio of industrial sales GDP rose from 90 per cent in 2002 to 140 per cent in 2005. Further, this industrial expansion was concentrated primarily in heavy industries—materials (steel, cement, aluminium), machinery, and chemicals.[38] The recent expansion of heavy industries has spilled over into the trade surplus.

Up to 2004, the trade balance was fairly stable at 1.7 per cent of GDP (see Chart 6.15 above). There was sharp spike thereafter—4.5 per cent in 2005, 6.8 per cent in 2006, and a projected 9 per cent–10 per cent in 2007 (see Chart 6.16 and Chart 6.17). The abrupt expansion of the trade surplus after 2004 can be explained by two factors: First, the expansion of heavy industries sector exports. These are largely 'commoditized materials', like steel, cement,

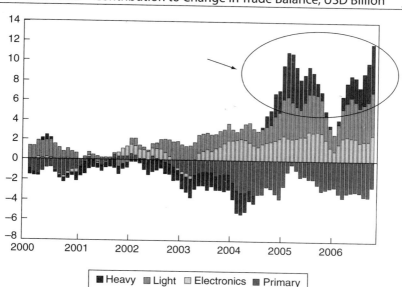

Chart 6.15   Contribution to Change in Trade Balance, USD Billion

■ Heavy ■ Light □ Electronics ■ Primary

Source: Jonathan Anderson, 'Solving China's Rebalancing Puzzle', *Finance and Development*, IMF, Volume 44, Number 3, September 2007.

Chart 6.16   Soaring Trade Surpluses

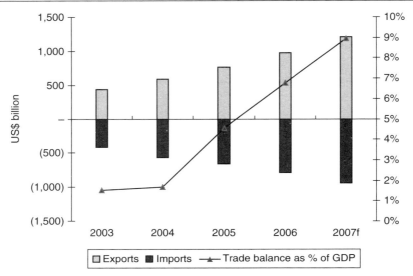

(f = forecast)
Source: *China Economic Quarterly*, 2007 Q2

Chart 6.17   Is China De-linking from the East Asian Division of Labour?

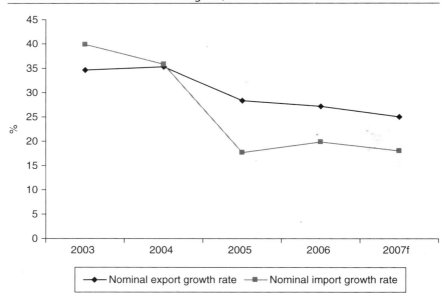

(f = forecast)
Source: *China Economic Quarterly*, 2007 Q2

and aluminium. To be sure, China's heavy-machinery industry has upgraded its indigenous capabilities. Consequently, heavy machinery's trade balance has improved from a trade deficit of US$ 39 billion in 2003 to a surplus of US$ 9.7 billion in the first half of 2007. Second, there has probably been an increasing share of localization of previously imported components, as MNCs' production networks have relocated to the mainland. Indeed, FDI growth rate jumped from 1.4 per cent in 2003 to 13.3 per cent in 2004 and 19.5 per cent in 2005. A combination of both these factors, perhaps, accounts for the divergence in export–import growth rates after 2004, although both have grown slower since 2004.

Some economists have pointed out that this rapidly growing trade surplus along with the substitution of imports with locally produced components represents a trend toward China defecting from the East Asian supply chains and a crowding out of other regional economies.[39] However, such an inference, so far, is empirically unjustified.

First, such a perception fails to capture the complexity of the vertically integrated value chains, where cross-border investment flows are equally critical to the evolution of geo-economic linkages among East Asian economies (see Chapter 5). East Asian economies seeking efficiency gains (and market access) are relocating some parts of their components production to mainland China's expanding value-added production base, and thereby slowing the growth of bilateral exports to China, but more importantly, also exporting more sophisticated components. Simultaneously, China has also emerged as a source for relatively low-value machinery components. Such components are imported by South East Asian economies, processed further, and often shipped back to mainland China for final assembly. In sum, there are positive externalities for the East Asian production-sharing network as China expands its manufacturing base.[40]

Importantly, FIEs still account for a large portion of China's electronic-processing exports. For the period January–August 2007, FIEs accounted for 67 per cent of the total export volume of electronic-information products.[41] Further, the value add of China's electronic-information manufactures was around 22 per cent for the same period, suggesting that China is still heavily reliant on imported components. Thus, trade statistics alone cannot wholly explain the pattern of interdependence.[42]

Second, the expansion of China's trade surplus since 2004 is also driven by an expansion in certain heavy-industry sectors that have less to do with processing-type exports and perhaps more to do with a cyclical overcapacity that has spilled over into the trade surplus.

'STRUCTURAL REBALANCING'

The overall macroeconomic imperative of sustaining an externally driven growth model has also manifested in Beijing's behaviour in exchange-rate policies and its reluctance to float the yuan, since, by capital controls, domestic savings are held captive for internal federal use, and a competitive exchange rate is simultaneously maintained to buttress the export orientation of the Chinese economy. However, a rapidly expanding current-account surplus over the past three years now projected at over 10 per cent of GDP for 2007[43] has re-altered Beijing's calculus. According to the 11th Five Year plan (2006–11), Beijing has signalled its intention to rebalance growth by focusing on domestic demand. To some extent, the exchange rate would then become a useful tool to bring about the proposed 'expenditure switching' in China's economy.[44]

However, the pace of such an adjustment will depend on the success of financial-sector reforms in China, as Beijing's planners are unlikely to float the yuan before the financial system can assume the role of a sophisticated intermediary. In fact, the yuan has been appreciating vis à vis the dollar—by 2 per cent in 2005, 4 per cent in 2006 and 6 per cent year-on-year by August 2007. Moreover, expected inflation (ADB forecast) of 4.2 per cent in 2007 and 3.8 per cent in 2008 implies a real appreciation of the yuan anyway. Yet, the impact of reducing exports has so far been limited, given Chinese firms' success in passing through the higher prices to their export markets.[45] Seeking more effective measures to rein in exports, Beijing has imposed selective export tariffs and withdrawn export-tax rebates.[46] In terms of fiscal measures, Beijing has increased the share of spending on education, health, and social security to 27 per cent of the total federal budget. This could reduce the 'precautionary saving' incentive for rural households and, thereby, augment private consumption. Insofar as the SOE sector is concerned, economists have pointed out that Beijing could speed up the process of extracting dividend payments to reduce retained earning and, thus, slow down investment (recall 'self-financing' has been the primary source of investment). Finally, China could also raise the cost of capital in sectors that are facing cyclical overcapacity to discourage further investment.

In aggregate, one can unequivocally state that given the extent of China's integration into economic globalization, it is remarkable that it has sustained both dynamic growth and ensured a reasonable degree of economic security.[47] China's strong internal and external macroeconomic balances implies unlike India, it possesses the fiscal strength to stimulate internal demand in a scenario of a pronounced global slowdown, an ability already demonstrated both during the Asian financial crisis and in response to the global recession in 2001. China's diversification of its export portfolio and success in tapping new foreign markets in recent years implies that it is now emerging as a driver for global growth in its own right. Furthermore, while property rights and related institutions were far from the ideal textbook case, the fundamental ingredients of China's reform strategy was in sync with the success of her East Asian peers—education, high savings, and export orientation.

After 25 years of reforms, as Beijing's focus evolves from solely focusing on mobilizing unemployed resources and correcting structural bottlenecks toward optimizing efficiency in the allocation of China's capital, the evolution of China's financial infrastructure and banking sector assumes critical salience.[48]

POLICY LESSONS FOR INDIA

Since India, too, seeks to deepen and widen its integration with the global economic system, the lessons from its northern neighbour may perhaps be too relevant to ignore. For New Delhi to exploit broader growth opportunities via FDI and trade, and simultaneously ensure the negative aspects of globalization are mitigated, and particularly those that may impinge upon the foreign policy autonomy of New Delhi, it will need to carefully weigh the cost-benefits of particular policy choices and calibrate its liberalization process.

The limits of the prevailing services-led growth structure have been recognized. Since information-technology-related exports (i.e., IT/ITES) represent only 6 per cent of the service-sector output, extremely high growth would be required to sustain the imbalance between the goods and the services account.[49] Moreover, the sustainability of such a high export-growth strategy can prove elusive, given the emergence of competing outsourcing centres among low-wage countries (especially Vietnam and Philippines) and local supply-side bottlenecks within India. Thus, India must seek to diversify its export base.

According to the United Nations, between 2005 and 2025, the working-age population in India will expand by approximately 273 million. The country's total population will rise by 313 million over this period. Indeed, the Planning Commission itself has noted that India will need to generate 200 million additional jobs by 2020.[50] In the near-term, 71 million young

Indians, which includes 45 million rural youth, will enter the workforce by 2010. Thus, with an average of 13 million people expected to enter India's labour force each year for the next four decades, economists have expressed concerns about the relatively jobless growth of the last 15 years.[51]

In sum, skill-based development in the Indian socio-economic context offers little prospect for national employment growth. According to NASSCOM, a leading public policy platform for the IT industry, India's IT and BPO sector will only account for 8.8 million jobs (mainly urban educated) by 2010. The remainder 88 per cent or 62 million jobs can only be created by expanding the manufacturing sector.

The fact that India's slowest-growing states are also its most populated greatly exacerbates the development challenge. The share of four BIMARU states—Bihar, Madhya Pradesh, Rajasthan and Uttar Pradesh—of India's population is projected to rise from 41 per cent in 2001 to 48 per cent in 2051. The average growth rate of GDP for the BIMARU states for the period 1992–2002 was 4.5 per cent. Thus, 60 per cent of India's population increment will be concentrated in these four states.

Such a socio-economic structure would imply increasing the share of tradable low-skilled, labour-intensive manufacturing industries in overall output, and diversifying the current specialization in skill-based production, which itself is now facing formidable supply-side constraints,[52] for this is the only feasible path to leveraging the massive labour surplus in India.

Finally, the linkage between manufacturing-led industrialization and the development of a robust military-industrial complex implies that 'bypassing' such a vital stage of economic development will deny India the capacity to autonomously develop capabilities and successfully absorb high-end military technologies over the long run. To be sure, India's 'strategic enclaves'—DRDO, ISRO, DAE—have managed to establish a modest military-industrial complex in the absence of wider civil-industrial contribution, though India's import dependence on external military technologies is still overwhelming (over 70 per cent). Thus, the existing policy is unlikely to be sustainable in the medium to long term. In sum, India cannot reinvent the wheel in this crucial sphere!

'We wish to emulate China in the matter of infrastructure.'—Indian Finance Minister, February 2007

China's infrastructure development was closely linked to the FDI-driven export strategy. This is something India must seek to emulate, given the dual objective of increasing exports and providing infrastructure, especially since the former can hardly take-off without successfully addressing the latter challenge. To be sure, India did approve legislation for establishing special economic zones (SEZs) in 2005. However, as T. N. Srinivasan notes, some of the crucial features of China's zones, such as allowing 100 per cent foreign ownership, freedom of firms to hire and fire workers, and the provision of robust transport and communications infrastructure are missing in India's zones. There are still sectoral caps for FDI. Exemption from draconian labour laws has been left to the states.[53] Thus, while overall FDI in India is growing, FDI in manufacturing actually declined in 2006 to US$ 1.5bn, compared with US$ 1.8bn in 2005, reflecting the fact that the environment for manufacturing FDI is not yet attractive enough.[54] Chart 6.18 below illustrates the share of infrastructure spending by India considered for the next five years.

According to New Delhi's recent, integrated energy report, for the economy to maintain its present growth rate, India will have to expand electricity production from the present level of 131,000 megawatts to as much as 900,000 megawatts by 2020.[55] Nirvikar Singh at the University of California, in a recent analysis of input–output structure, identified 10 leading sectors in the Indian economy based on growth impacts on GDP of efficiency improvements in these sectors. These sectors include—electricity, water and gas supply, transport services, railway-transport services, coal and lignite, etc. He found that India's growth rate is at least as sensitive to these sectors as it was prior to the 1991 reforms.[56] This again brings back a point made in Chapter 4. Unlike China, which at the onset of reforms, decoupled its inefficient state sector with the construction of new tax-free trade zones in its eastern coastal

Chart 6.18   Envisaged Share of Infrastructure Spending for the Next Five Years

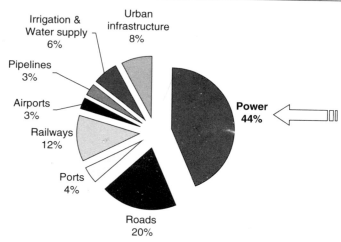

Source: Centre for Policy Alternatives Research, New Delhi.

provinces, India's 'integrated' structure implies that a dynamic private component of GDP is intrinsically linked to state-dominated, underinvested, infrastructure sectors.

That supply-side constraints are already threatening macroeconomic
growth is clear from India's relatively high level of capacity utilization vis à vis
her BRIC peers, suggesting overheating pressures (see Chart 6.19).

Chart 6.19 above clearly shows that India is operating close to peak
capacity, and rapid investment is required to alleviate systemic bottlenecks.
Indeed, the RBI's 2007 annual report clearly states that sustainable growth
would require infrastructure spending by both the public and private sectors needs to increase from the current levels of 4.6 per cent of GDP to
almost 8 per cent of GDP per annum.[57] Again, it must be reiterated that the
extent of China's investment in building supply-side capacities has been the
principal reason for its sustained inflation-free growth for over two decades.
In China's case, improved labour-market flexibility over the last decade has
further contained wage inflation.

First, it is clear that given the existing fiscal burdens, the state does not
possess the surpluses necessary to address the national-infrastructure deficit.
Public–private partnerships are an alternative, which have hitherto seen

Chart 6.19   Capacity Utilization for BRIC Economies, Quarterly 2005–2007

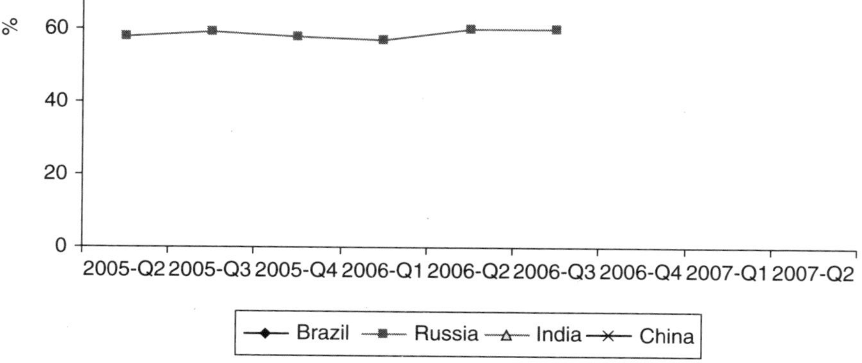

Source: Main Economic Indicators, OECD, August 2007

mixed results, largely on account of the varying spectrum of returns available in the infrastructure industries. Perhaps, the combination of 'export promotion' incentives by both the central and state governments, can aid in channelling resources toward green-field investments in infrastructure expansion itself, which would otherwise suffer from the usual 'free rider' problem. Indeed, the current SEZ policy appears to seek such a solution.

INFRASTRUCTURE—THE SPOILER

India needs an investment of Rs 12.7 trillion (US$ 317 bn @40INR/USD) over the next five years. The RBI recently stated that infrastructure spending by both the public and private sectors needed to increase from the current levels of 4.6 per cent of GDP to almost 8 per cent of GDP every year (see Chart 6.20 and Table 6.1).

India, similar to China, could focus on FDI in export sectors and seek to attract initially, the labour-intensive industries or sub-sectors that are gradually losing competitiveness in China, where resources are moving up the manufacturing value chain. Again, as in China, where the FDI that came in also had an incentive to create a 'parallel' infrastructure in the emerging coastal regions of the east, India by adopting appropriate policy incentives can imitate such a dual-policy goal.

Chart 6.20   Breakdown of Financing: Private Investment—Principal Contributor

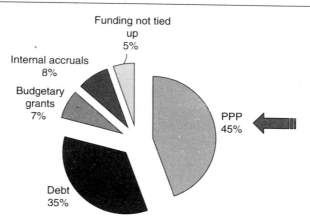

Source: Centre for Policy Alternatives Research, New Delhi.

Table 6.1 Infrastructure Spending by Sector

Rs bn	Budgetary grant	Debt				Privatization/ BOT	Funding not tied up	Total	Construction component	
		Multi lateral borrowing	Market borrowing	Internal Accruals	Sub-Total				%	Rs bn
Power	265	270	2,353	384	3,271	2,245	–	5,516	43	2,349
Roads	228	186	123	–	537	1,857	80	2,474	100	2,474
Ports	38	75	50	50	213	345	–	558	60	335
Railways	75	50	120	350	595	300	600	1,495	42	628
Airports	10	25	25	25	85	300	15	400	42	168
Pipelines	–	–	250	150	400	–	–	400	40	160
Irrigation & Water supply	226	206	321	8	761	25	–	786	45	354
Urban infra	97	295	58	60	510	521	–	1,031	60	619
Total	**938**	**1,107**	**3,301**	**1,027**	**6,373**	**5,593**	**695**	**12,660**	**56**	**7,086**

Source: Centre for Policy Alternatives Research, New Delhi.

India, in contrast to China, remains relatively a 'closed' economy where indigenous sources of growth (i.e., consumption) have been the primary drivers of the economic story. The infrastructure deficit has ensured that supply-side bottlenecks continue to stifle manufacturing and export potential. 'Infrastructure' here also includes economic infrastructure services, such as education and healthcare, which are vital lifelines, if India is to exploit its so-called demographic dividend. China's success in ensuring educational attainment has been an important factor in both labour reallocations away from agriculture as well as sustaining productivity growth (see Chart 6.21). In an earlier chapter, we alluded to India's distorted education policy where the focus on its massive lower and middle layer has been perfunctory.[58] Until this aspect is comprehensively addressed, in partnership with private participation, India would find it structurally impossible to transform itself from an agrarian to industrial society (see Chart 6.22).

India, accounted for about 2 per cent in the growth of world exports and imports over the period 1995–2004, and its most dynamic export sector is information technology (IT)-enabled services (see Chart 6.23 and Chart 6.24). However, India's manufacturing exports are starting to grow strongly, particularly in textiles and clothing as well as the pharmaceuticals

Chart 6.21   Educational Attainment of the Total Population Aged 15–64, 2000

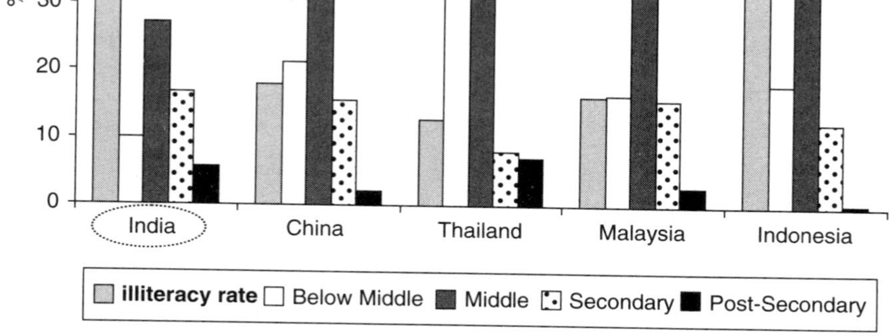

Legend: illiteracy rate ☐ Below Middle ■ Middle ☒ Secondary ■ Post-Secondary

Source: Barry Bosworth, Susan M. Collins, Arvind Virmani, 'Sources of Growth in the Indian Economy', NBER Working Paper 12901, Cambridge, MA, February 2007.

Chart 6.22   India's Education Distribution by Sectors, 2004

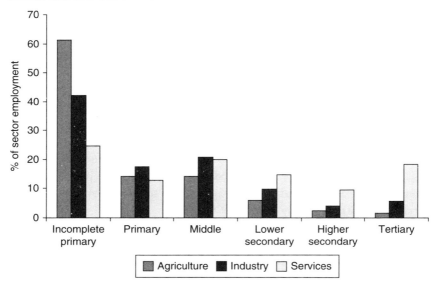

Source: India National Sample Survey Organization, Socio-Economic Survey, Round 60, January–June 2004, *Asian Development Outlook 2007*

Chart 6.23   Asian Export Ratio

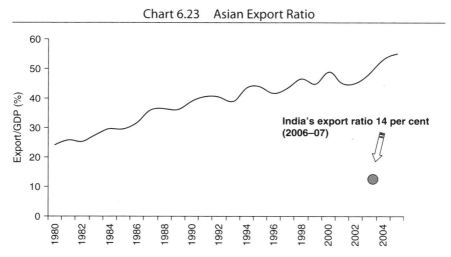

India's export ratio 14 per cent (2006–07)

Source: Oxford Economics, Quarterly Model, February 2007.
Note: Asia comprises People's Republic of China, Hong Kong, Indonesia, Republic of Korea, Malaysia, Philippines, Singapore, Taipei, and Thailand.

Chart 6.24   Share in World Trade, 1990–2004 (Per Cent)

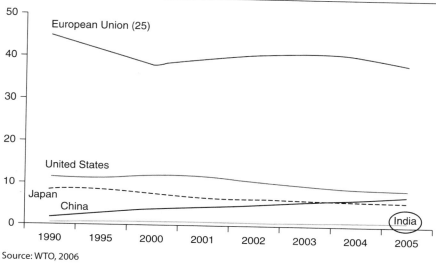

Source: WTO, 2006

sectors. But India needs to further exploit the role of the external sector as a vital growth engine, and importantly, enter the growing trade in manufactured parts and components that has characterised intra-East Asian commerce. The Asian Development Bank recently noted, 'Though exports are now growing quickly in some countries of South Asia, it has not yet latched onto international production networks to the same degree as East Asia'.[59] In fact, South Asia is the least integrated region in the world. Intraregional trade accounts for just 5 per cent of total trade, while for East Asia, the ratio is 55 per cent.

PSU Reforms: If there is one major comparative lesson that can be drawn from the Chinese experience, it is that given India's political economy, sector-wise deepening of private-sector expansion in India need not come at the expense of the PSU incumbents, which also happen to be the primary suppliers of infrastructure goods and services. Indeed, this utility of approach is now empirically vindicated after the adverse policy lessons of the 'shock therapy' experience in the post-Soviet CIS and Latin America, where state enterprises were stripped of assets to reallocate resources to the private sector. Besides, such a policy is unnecessary for India, which similar to China has a massive endowment of underemployed labour surplus, and hence does not need resources from the PSUs to be redeployed. What is required is a systemic overhaul of the incentive structure, facing the Indian PSUs. Thus, parallel-track industrial reforms, which focus on reforming, restructuring and creating greater autonomy for PSUs (as China has sought to execute for the central SOEs via SASAC) along with improved anti-trust regulation for private-sector activity. Telecom Regulatory Authority of India (TRAI) is an excellent example of an Indian regulator that reconciled its mandate to promote competition, preserving the viability and interests of the two major PSUs (BSNL, MTNL) (see Appendix for a policy brief on critical relevance of anti-trust in India).

EXCHANGE-RATE POLICY

China's exchange-rate policies have not been dissimilar to India's case of a 'managed float'. However, recently, the RBI's attitude has witnessed a move toward greater currency movement because of easing capital controls. Yet, given India's superior financial-market reforms, the Ministry of Finance and the RBI are perhaps in a better position to allow the rupee to fluctuate. But the important theme that is relevant here is whether an appreciating rupee assists in the larger strategic economic goal of export-oriented industrialization.[60]

By August 2007, the rupee had appreciated by over 10 per cent against the US dollar.[61] The costs of this avoidable rupee appreciation are manifesting in the economic data: marked slowdown in exports of goods and services, sudden pressure from cheap imports on import-substituting activities, rising job losses in labour-using industries like textiles, and sharply mounting trade deficits. In a recent critique, one Indian economist notes that 'keeping the exchange rate undervalued provides huge benefits to the economy, benefits that are more than 6 times the cost for India, and more than 11 times the cost for China'.[62] Another economist notes that 'the push to attract more foreign capital appears to be taking place without giving much thought about how much the economy can absorb without creating challenges for monetary policy, and about the approximate level where the exchange rate becomes a political liability'.[63]

In aggregate, an appreciating rupee then is merely another reflection of India's 'insular' economy, where the domestic market (as the primary driver for growth) gains by cheaper imports and fuels local demand, and increased capital inflows. In the longer run, however, such an approach runs contrary to the overall strategic economic policy that we have sought to endorse here—namely, the importance of expanding the tradable manufacturing sector's share in the overall GDP growth. With an already prevailing manufacturing trade deficit, an appreciating rupee will further stifle the growth of employment-generating, low-technology manufacturing sectors. Moreover, aside from deepening socio-economic development internally, such an industrial-oriented economic policy will simultaneously enhance India's linkages with different actors, thereby increasing its regional influence.

According to the 'impossible trinity', a country can choose between the following options:

1. A fixed exchange rate with a lack of an autonomous interest-rate policy and free capital mobility,

2. An autonomous interest-rate policy with a freely floating exchange rate and free capital mobility,

3. Capital controls and a combination of a fixed exchange rate and an autonomous interest-rate policy.

It may be noted that both China and India have adopted what can be called a 'low-speculation fixed but adjustable regime'[64], where both have sought to impose a degree of capital control on short-term capital movements (they did not interfere with non-hot money investment driven flows—FDI, portfolio investments). This has enabled them to sustain a largely fixed exchange rate and a monetary (interest rate) policy independent of the exchange-rate policy. Moreover, the rapid accumulation of foreign exchange reserves and low short-term debt-to-reserve ratios in both countries since the Asian financial crisis has made such an exchange-rate-stabilization policy credible (note; that India's fixed-rate commitment was relatively less rigid).

India's seems to be currently between 3 and 2, but gradual capital-account liberalization is pressuring it toward 2. This is precisely the dilemma facing the RBI for the last few years. As India's external account has been liberalized (to enable greater capital inflows) the exchange rate is gradually getting market determined and the RBI is losing absolute control over the exchange-rate movements. Economists have pointed out the financial costs of Indian sterilization that stem from the positive domestic–foreign interest-rate differential in the Indian case. Thus, the RBI, while absorbing foreign exchange reserves, would also by selling bonds accumulate domestic liabilities whose interest-rate costs are higher than returns on its foreign-asset holdings. But as economists point out, this cost is negligible. The total amount in the stabilization scheme today is around US\$ 22 billion. Total loss due to interest costs, at a maximum of 3 per cent per annum, is US\$ 660 million, which for India's US\$ 1 trillion dollar GDP, is only 0.66 per cent of GDP. In sum, benefits

Table 6.2   Cost–Benefit Analysis of Currency Intervention

Benefits outweigh the costs of currency management	India	China
GDP (in US$ billions), in 2000	460	1200
GDP (in US$ billions), in 2006	880	2560
Level of Reserves (in US$ billions), in 2006	220	1300
Level of Reserves (In US$ billions), in 2000	41	172
Level of currency undervaluation in 2000 (%)	−11	−18
Level of currency undervaluation in 2006 (%)	−28	−56
Per year average change in undervaluation, 2000–2006, %	−2.8	−6.3
Maximum loss from undervaluation 2000 to 2006	6.6	−2.2
Loss due to sterilization (@ 3% per annum of Accumulated reserves) (For China, a benefit since interest rates are 1 per cent lower than the US)		
Loss due to possible appreciation of domestic currency (@3% per annum)	6.6	39
Total loss from accumulation of reserves	13.2	36.8
Gains from undervaluation (via higher GDP growth)	460	1200
Gain in GDP, 2000 to 2006, from low initial (2000) undervaluation (@ −.02*initial GDP*initial undervaluation) for 6 years	27.0	158.8
Gain in GDP (2000 to 2006) from change in undervaluation since initial years		
(@ −.35*initial GDP*avg. change in undervaluation each year for 6 years	87.8	418.0
Total gain in GDP from currency undervaluation for 6 years (US$ billion)		
addition of gains fro level and change in undervaluation	6.6	11.4
Benefit/cost ratio (ratio of total gains/total losses)		

Source: Surjit S. Bhalla, 'Second Among Equals: The Middle Class Kingdoms of India and China', Peterson Institute of International Economics, draft May 2007.

of exchange-rate management are more than 6 times the cost for India, and more than 11 times the cost for China[65] (see Table 6.2).

China, it may be reiterated, has strategically sought to stay at option 3, electing a fixed exchange rate and an independent monetary policy (with capital controls), thereby, electing to sterilize foreign-exchange inflows on a massive scale. Further, insofar as there is a positive interest-rate differential between US T-bills (that comprise China's reserves) and China's domestic real-interest rate, Beijing has been able to actually profit during its phase of currency management![66]

Agriculture lags behind with adverse socio-economic consequences, given its disproportionate share of rural employment. According to the RBI's 2007 annual report, 'volatility in agricultural production has not only implications for overall growth but also, as the experience of 2006–07 amply demonstrated, for maintaining low and stable inflation. Enhanced growth of the agricultural sector is vital for ensuring food security, poverty alleviation, price stability, overall inclusive growth and sustainability of growth of the overall economy'.[67] In fact, the agricultural sector has been facing a structural demise—growth decelerated from an annual average of 4.7 per cent per year during the 1980s to 3.1 per cent during the 1990s and further to 2.2 per cent in the 2000s. (In contrast, China's agricultural sector continues to grow at over 4 per cent, despite entering its thirtieth year of the post-reform era in 2008). India's woes have been attributed to 'declining investment, lack of proper irrigation facilities, other inadequate infrastructural facilities, inadequate attention to R&D for developing high-yielding varieties of seeds, absence of major technological breakthroughs, improper use of fertilizers and institutional weaknesses'.[68]

Services contributed 69 per cent of the overall average growth in GDP in the last 5 years between 2002–03 and 2006–07. The residual contribution came largely from industry. As a result, in 2006–07, while the share of agriculture in GDP declined to 18.5 per cent, the share of industry improved to marginally 26.4 per cent and services to 55.1 per cent.

The figures in Table 6.3 clearly indicate the supply-side constraints imposed by the relatively lower growth in infrastructure sectors (mining, electricity, water supply, etc.), which, if addressed, can spur industrial growth—particularly manufacturing.

'Both savings and investment as proportion of GDP must be raised further.'—Indian Finance Minister, February 2007

INVESTMENT NEEDS SAVINGS

Gross-domestic-capital formation (GDCF) has always outstripped gross domestic saving (GDS) in India (except for a brief spell 2001–2003, when India recorded a current-account surplus). The implied dependence on foreign savings (i.e., saving–investment gap) was lower in the 1990s as compared to that in the 1980s, indicating an improvement in the current-account deficit during the 1990s and a commensurate decline in the dependence on foreign saving. Sector-wise analysis of saving–investment gaps, on the other hand, indicates that the household sector experienced a steady surplus. While both the public and private corporate sectors were in deficit during the 1980s and 1990s, the saving–investment gap of the public sector was higher than that of the private corporate sector (see Chart 6.25).

Table 6.3 Sectoral Growth Rates in GDP at Factor Cost (1999–2000 Prices)

Item	Percentage change over the previous year						
	2000–01	2001–02	2002–03	2003–04	2004–05	2005–06 (Q)	2006–07 (A)
I. Agriculture & allied	**–0.2**	**6.3**	**–7.2**	**10.0**	**0.0**	**6.0**	**2.7**
II. Industry	**6.4**	**2.7**	**7.1**	**7.4**	**9.8**	**9.6**	**10.0**
Mining and quarrying	2.4	1.8	8.8	3.1	7.5	3.6	4.5
Manufacturing	7.7	2.5	6.8	6.6	8.7	9.1	11.3
Electricity, gas & water supply	2.1	1.7	4.7	4.8	7.5	5.3	7.7
Construction	6.2	4.0	7.9	12.0	14.1	14.2	9.4
III. Services	**5.7**	**7.2**	**7.4**	**8.5**	**9.6**	**9.8**	**11.2**
Trade, hotels, transport and communication	7.3	9.1	9.2	12.1	10.9	10.4	13.0
Financial, real estate & business services	4.1	7.3	8.0	5.6	8.7	10.9	11.1
Community, social and personal services	4.8	4.1	3.9	5.4	7.9	7.7	7.8
IV. Total GDP at factor cost	**4.4**	**5.8**	**3.8**	**8.5**	**7.5**	**9.0**	**9.2**

P: Provisional   **Q: Quick**   **A: Advance estimates**

Source: Central Statistical Organisation.

Chart 6.25   The Change of the Composition of India's Saving and Investment
            Rates over Time

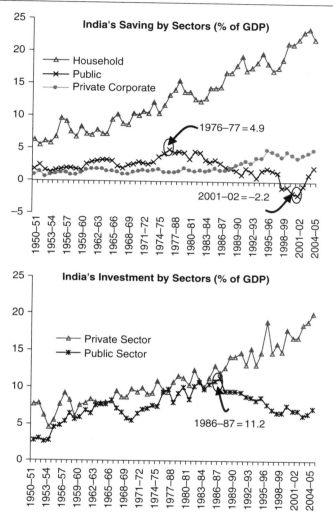

Source: Deepak Mishra, 'Can India Attain the East Asian Growth with South Asian Saving Rate?', World Bank, July 2006.

Following the liberalization of the Indian economy in 1991, the public sector has gradually withdrawn from a number of sectors, whose place has been taken over by the private sector. This, along with the fact that India's current expenditure grew rapidly while its revenue collection stagnated, resulting in more than 10 per cent of general government deficit during the 1990s, explains why public investment declined during this period. From financing 50 per cent to 55 per cent of total investment in the economy in the early 1980s, the government's share fell to around 5 per cent by the early 2000s. With fiscal deficit on a declining trend in recent years, public saving has again turned positive.

Comparison of the saving rate of India and China puts the overall long-term prospects for growth in perspective:

Indian households are found to save more than their Chinese counterparts, while India's corporate and public savings are considerably lower than the corresponding numbers in China. In fact, there is a wide 15–18 percentage point difference between enterprise saving in China and private corporate saving in India, which accounts for bulk of the difference in the aggregate saving between the two countries (see Chart 6.26). In China, household saving to GDP ratio has fallen, though stable, for the last five years, which has been more than offset by the increase in enterprise and public-sector saving to GDP ratio (this is consistent with our earlier discussion on corporate sector driving the saving investment boom in China). In India, household saving fell in 2004–05, and the subsequent analysis seems to point towards a tapering off of India's household saving rate in the near term (as has already happened in China).

At the outset, the need for higher savings arises from the stated objective of expanding into more capital-intensive, manufacturing-driven industrialization. For example, simply infrastructure investment itself implies higher capital intensity. For instance, capital intensity of the electricity, gas, and water sub-sectors is nearly three times that of the business-services sector. Note that thus far, the primary driver of Indian growth has been the services sector, which relies on less capital per unit of output (i.e., growth has been less capital intensive than it would have been, had India relied on manufacturing-led growth, implying a lower capital-output ratio (see Chart 6.27).

India can increase the available capital for investment by a combination of two strategies. First, increase the level of its domestic savings and channel them efficiently. Second, run a current-account deficit (capital-account surplus) to draw in external savings to finance growth. Yet, we have noted that the second option has adverse implications on the exchange rate, which run counter to the export-driven development that India seeks to achieve. Thus, mobilizing internal savings both by fiscal consolidation and efficient capital allocation by the intermediary banking sector is likely to yield robust saving

Chart 6.26   Comparison of India's Saving Rate with That of Other East Asian Countries

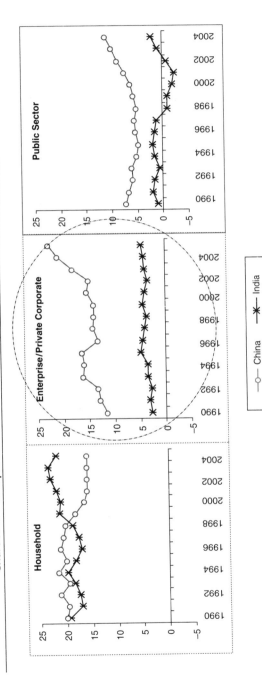

Source: Deepak Mishra, 'Can India Attain the East Asian Growth with South Asian Saving Rate?', World Bank, July 2006.

Chart 6.27   Capital Output Ratio

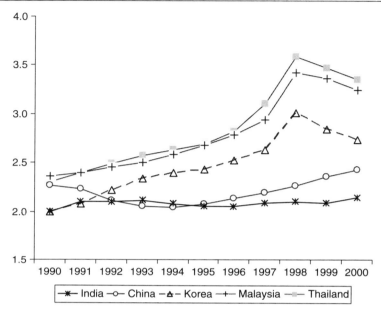

Source: Deepak Mishra, 'Can India Attain the East Asian Growth with South Asian Saving Rate?', World Bank, July 2006.

rates to finance long-term growth. Insofar as the favourable demographic structure (i.e., falling age-dependency ratio) will further buttress household saving rates, it is another positive variable in ensuring growth can be financed by indigenous capital.

According to a Mckinsey report, households invest just half of their savings in bank deposits (see Chart 6.28). Further, Indian banks lend only 61 per cent of their deposits, roughly half the G-7 average. The remainder of bank deposits, around 33 per cent, gets channelled in government securities. Finally, India's corporate-bond market is still nascent (i.e., 2 per cent of GDP).[69] Thus, further financial-sector reforms will increase the size of India's financial system, which is so vital in ensuring that savings are allocated efficiently and quickly.

Thus, the state in India, similar to China, also dominates the banking system (see Chart 6.29), with 70 per cent of surplus savings channelled through the financial system going into India's public sector. We noted earlier how such a system of 'financial repression' in China created massive demand

Chart 6.28 Breakdown of Household Savings in India

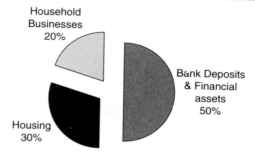

Source: 'Accelerating India's Growth Through Financial System Reform', McKinsey, May 2006

Chart 6.29 Share of Bank Loans, India

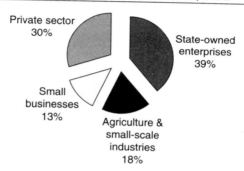

Source: 'Accelerating India's Growth Through Financial System Reform', McKinsey, May 2006

pull for external capital in the form of FDI. For structural and business environment reasons, India was unable to receive significant FDI. However, we also noted that in China's case, corporate-sector savings ('self-financing') is the primary financier of investment. This appears to be the case for India's private sector as well. The shares of sources of funds in the private sector in India have been represented in Chart 6.30.

The savings ratio has increased from 26.4 per cent in 2002–03 to 32.4 per cent in 2005–06, largely driven by private corporate savings (see Chart 6.31). In sum, the additional resources that have sustained the resurgence in economic growth in the past four years have largely come outside of the household sector—from company earnings and budgetary gains[70], similar to China. With rising gross domestic savings between 2003–04 and 2004–05, there was a step up in the rate of gross domestic capital formation

Chart 6.30   Private Sector: Sources of Funds, 2000–2005

Source: 'Accelerating India's Growth through Financial System Reform', McKinsey, May 2006

Chart 6.31   Composition of National Savings Rate

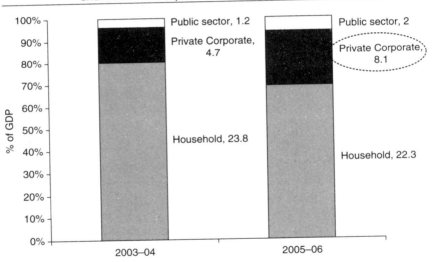

Source: RBI Annual Report, Appendix Table 11, 2006–07.

(GDCF) from 28 per cent of GDP to 31.5 per cent of GDP leading to a saving–investment gap or a current-account deficit of 0.4 per cent of GDP in 2004–05. GDCF rose further to 33.8 per cent of GDP in 2005–06 as per the quick estimates, widening the saving–investment gap to 1.4 per cent of GDP, with its implications for the current account.

NOTES

1   James Riedel, Jing Jin, and Jian Gao, *How China Grows: Investment, Finance, and Reform*, New Jersey: Princeton University Press, 2007.

2   Ibid, p. 38.

3   Steven Barnett and Ray Brooks, 'What's Driving Investment in China?', IMF Working Paper, November 2006.

4   Source: NBS historical data, *China Economic Quarterly* (CEQ) forecasts.

5   Hong Liang, 'China's Investment Strength Is Sustainable', Global Economics Paper No: 146, Goldman Sachs, 3 October 2006.

6   Chong-En Bai, Chang-Tai Hsieh, and Yingyi Qian, 'The Return to Capital in China', NBER Working Paper No. 12755, Cambridge, MA, December 2006).

7   'China's Investment: Dim Sums', *The Economist*, 2 November 2006.

8   Hong Liang, 'China's Investment Strength Is Sustainable', Global Economics Paper No: 146, Goldman Sachs, 3 October 2006; Jonathan Anderson, 'Solving China's Rebalancing Puzzle', *Finance and Development*, IMF, Volume 44, Number 3, September 2007. Also See Louis Kuijs, 'Investment and Saving in China', World Bank Policy Research Working Paper 3633, June 2005.

9   Again, according to the World Bank's *China Quarterly Update, May 2007*, recent developments suggest that there is no widespread overcapacity in China's industry. Profitability and profit-growth developments have been favourable. Indeed, some of the sectors, including steel, that were not too long ago identified as having overcapacity, enjoyed record profit increases in the first quarter of 2007.

10 Taye Mengistae, Lixin Colin Xu, Bernard Yeung, 'China vs. India: A Microeconomic Look at Comparative Macroeconomic Performance', World Bank Background Paper, May 2006.

11 In addition, since around 58 per cent of all imports into the USA come from US subsidiaries operating in China, this further reduces incentives in the USA to restrict Chinese exports.

12 'Economics Focus, "An Old Chinese Myth"', *The Economist*, 3 January 2008.

13 Dani Rodrik, 'What's So Special About China's Exports?', NBER Working Paper 11947, National Bureau of Economic Research, Cambridge, MA, 2006.

14 According to Airbus and Boeing, China is expected to become the world's second-biggest commercial aircraft market, after the United States by 2026, with airlines expected to buy 3,400 passenger and cargo planes worth US$ 340 billion in the next two decades.

15 'Assembly in China Vital for Sales, says Airbus', *Financial Times*, 6 September 2007; 'China Hopes a Home Grown Regional Jetliner can Challenge Airbus and Boeing', *International Herald Tribune*, 7 September 2007.

16   Mure Dickie, 'China Unveils State Aircraft Builder', *Financial Times*, 12 May 2008.

17   In 2003, this figure (employment in agriculture) had come down to 40 per cent.

18   This is sharp contrast to Russia and other CIS states that began their transition to marketization of their economies with about 90 per cent of the labour force employed in the state-owned sector. Consequently, these economies did not have surplus labour to reallocate to the newly created private sector. Of course, the 'big bang' policies of large-scale privatizations in the 1990s imposed severe political economy costs, which have only recently been reversed most dramatically by the reassertion of the Russian state.

19   'How China Grows', *Investment, Finance, and Reform*, 2007, p. 29.

20   See Ha-Joon Chang, *Globalisation, Economic Development and the Role of the State*, London: Zed Books, 2003. Also see Ha-Joon Chang, *Kicking Away the Ladder: Development Strategy in Historical Perspective*, London:Anthem Press, 2003—where in a historical survey the author illustrates that even the contemporary laissez faire economies in their early stages of development employed industrial policies uncannily similar to China, India and other emerging economies. Kokko (2002) provides a survey on how Japan used government intervention to promote 44 strategic industries including steel and shipbuilding. See Ari Kokko, 'Export-Led Growth In East Asia: Lessons For Europe's Transition Economies', Working Paper no. 142, Stockholm School of Economics, 2002. Finally, see Prem Shankar Jha, *The Perilous Road to the Market—The Political Economy of Reform in Russia, India, and China*, London: Pluto Press, 2002, for a rare comparative commentary on the transition experiences of three important Eurasian actors. Jha concludes that there can be no single strategy or set time frame for economic transition, and the state has a crucial role to play.

21   'How China Grows': *Investment, Finance, and Reform*, p. 40. It is also worth noting that SOEs employment in absolute terms still account for approximately 70 million jobs.

22   Hong Liang, 'China's Investment Strength Is Sustainable', Global Economics Paper No: 146, Goldman Sachs, 3 October 2006.

23   World Bank's *China Quarterly Update May 2006*.

24   Yongnian Zheng Minjia Chen, 'China's Recent SOE Reform and its Social Consequences', Briefing Series – Issue 23, China Policy Institute, University of Nottingham, June 2007.

25   Ibid.

26   Deputy Direct of SASAC: 'China Will Actively Promote the Reform of Personnel System in SOE', *Xinhua* news, 25 October 2006.

27   'SASAC: The State-Owned Economy Should Maintain Absolute Control in Seven Sectors', *Xinhua* news, 19 December 2006.

28   Lan Xinzhen, 'State Seeks Control of Critical Industries', www.beijingreview.com, 11 January 2007.

29   'SASAC Sets Rigid Target for Central SOEs', *China Daily*, 30 August 2007.

30   'Chinese Central SOEs Return 17 Bln Yuan from 2006 Profits', *Xinhua news*, 20 September 2007.

31   'Top 500 Enterprises 2007 Take Up 84 Per Cent of GDP', *China Daily*, 1 September 2007.

32   Zorawar Daulet Singh, 'Security: India Loses its Grip', *Asiatimes Online*, 21 December 2006; 'US Economic Slowdown Will Not Curb China's Growth', 26 November 2006, www.ResourceInvestor.com.

33   Lawrence Summers, 'Sovereign Funds Shake the Logic of Capitalism', *Financial Times*, 30 July 2007.

34   This is empirically underscored by the trend of global current account balances: In 1996, industrial economies ran a total current-account surplus of $41.5 billion compared to the total current-account deficit of US$ 90.4 billion by developing countries. By 2004, geo-economic patterns had reversed. Industrial economies ran a total deficit of US$ 400 billion (US$ 666 billion external deficit by the USA alone) versus developing economies (including China) that ran a current account surplus of US$ 327.4 billion.

35   'China Moves from Gatherer to Hunter', *Financial Times*, 22 August 2007; 'China Unveils Fund to Invest Forex Reserves', *Financial Times*, 29 September 2007.

36   Stephen Jen, 'How Big Could Sovereign Wealth Funds Be by 2015?', Morgan Stanley Research: Economics, 3 May 2007; Stephen Jen, 'Sovereign Wealth Funds and Official FX Reserves', Morgan Stanley Research: Economics, 14 September 2006.

37   Louis Kuijs and Song-Yi Kim, 'Raw Material Prices, Wages, and Profitability in China Industry: How was Profitability Maintained when Input Prices and Wages Increased So Fast?', World Bank China Research Paper No.8, October 2007.

38   Jonathan Anderson, 'Solving China's Rebalancing Puzzle', *Finance and Development*, IMF, Volume 44, Number 3, September 2007.

39   Andy Mukherjee, 'Asia Will Lose as "Made in China" Goes Local', www.bloomberg.com, 18 September 2007; Li Cui, 'China's Growing External Dependence', *Finance and Development*, IMF, Volume 44, Number 3, September 2007.

40   For instance, Taiwan's low-end manufacturing has largely relocated to mainland China.

   A recent World Bank paper finds that while China has increased its world market share in machinery exports, the author finds no evidence that China has squeezed the market shares of South East Asian machinery exports. Instead, components made by Southeast Asian countries are increasing in unit value and gaining market share in China. See Sjamsu Rahardja, 'Big Dragon, Little Dragons: China's Challenge to the Machinery Exports of Southeast Asia', Policy Research Working Paper 4297, The World Bank East Asia and Pacific Region Financial and Private Sector Unit, August 2007. Also see Mitsuyo Ando (Hitotsubashi University) and Fukunari Kimura (Keio University), 'Fragmentation in East Asia: Further Evidence', Hitotsubashi University, Tokyo, January 2007.

41   'China's Export of Electronic Info Products Up 26.2 Per Cent', *China Daily*, 2 October 2007.

42   Similar to US–China bilateral statistics, which exaggerate the extent of 'Chinese' exports.

43   China's trade surplus was around 2 per cent for 2000–2003, and 3 per cent in 2004.

44   'Switching' implies the effects of a real exchange-rate appreciation, which would reduce the relative prices of foreign vis à vis domestic goods, making the latter less competitive externally. This would then influence domestic resource allocation between tradable and non-tradable sectors—domestic consumers would consume more of the relatively cheaper imports, while domestic producers would reallocate resources toward the more profitable non-tradable sectors.

45   Jonathan Anderson, 'China Should Speed Up the Yuan's Rise', *The Far Eastern Economic Review*, July/August 2007.

46   From June 2007, an export tariff was imposed on 142 products, while export tax rebates were reduced or abolished in July 2007 for 2,831 items.

47   Beijing's approach to energy security exemplifies this point: Until 1993, half-way into its economic reforms, China was a net-exporter of hydrocarbons. Moreover, despite the subsequent scramble for overseas hydrocarbons, China has been able to maintain 90 per cent of overall energy supply via domestic sources.

48   James Riedel, Jing Jin, and Jian Gao, *How China Grows: Investment, Finance, and Reform*, New Jersey: Princeton University Press, 2007, p. 4.

   Note: Recently, Beijing's has begun to focus upon a 'harmonious development' reflecting the imperative to mitigate intra-regional disparity as well as seriously addressing the adverse environmental consequences of Chinese industrialization. This has also manifested in a recent policy of managing urbanization, which was signalled by the government's call for the construction of the 'new socialist countryside', perhaps indicating an intended slowdown in the urbanization process in the near future.

49   T. S. Papola, 'Emerging Structure of India Economy: Implications of Growing Inter-Sectoral Imbalances', Andhra University, Sec 27–29, 2005. Presidential Address, at the 88th Conference of Indian Economic Association. (The IT industry total revenues for FY 2007 are forecast at ~US$ 50 billion.)

50   Working age population (i.e., age 15–64 yrs.) will rise from 673 million in 2005 to 872 million in 2020.

51   'India's Pattern of Development: What Happened, What Follows?', IMF Working Paper, January 2006.

52   'India Inc. Facing Skilled Manpower Shortage: Survey', *Hindustan Times*, 8 July 2007; Amy Lee; 'Soaring Salaries to Hit India IT Margins', *Financial Times*, 12 September 2007.

53   T. N. Srinivasan, China, 'India and the World Economy', World Bank Working Paper No. 286, July 2006.

54   'Three Asian Giants', *The Economist*, 6 September 2007.

55   Pramit Pal Chaudhuri, 'India's Hydrocarbon Future', *Far Eastern Economic Review*, September 2007.

56   Nirvikar Singh, 'The Ten Sectors that Need a Boost', *Financial Express*, 12 December 2006.

57   'India's RBI says More Infrastructure Spend, Farm Output Needed to Sustain Growth', www.forbes.com, 30 August 2007.

58   We also noted that India's higher education system itself is facing enormous challenges.

59   *Asian Development Outlook 2007 Update.*

60   See the following articles on critiques of the RBI's evolving stance over exchange-rate management:, Shankar Acharya, 'Midsummer Madness?', *Business* Standard, 9 August 2007; Rajeev Malik, 'India's Handling of Rupee Remains a Riddle', 14 July 2007, www.rediff.com,; Surjit Bhalla, 'How India is Different from China', *Business* Standard, 18 August 2007; Surjit Bhalla, 'Rupee, Self-Interest and RBI Policy', *Business* Standard, 29 September 2007,.

61   On a trade-weighted basis, however, the rupee has been relatively stable.

62   Ibid, Bhalla.

63   Ibid, Malik.

64   W. Max Corden, *Too Sensational: On the Choice of Exchange Rate Regimes*, Cambridge, MA: MIT Press, 2002, pp. 42, 219–223. In a seminal analysis, the author extends the traditional focus of Western literature on exchange rate policies beyond the traditional bipolar choice—absolutely fixed or pure floating regimes—pro-offered to developing countries.

65   Surjit Bhalla, 'How India is Different from China: It Doesn't Matter', *Business Standard*, 18 August 2007.

66   It may be noted, that since July 2005, the Chinese yuan has been revalued by 14 per cent. People's Bank of China also raised interest rates 6 times in 2007, which has increased the cost of currency intervention.

67   RBI Press Release, 30 August 2007, http://rbi.org.in/scripts/BS_PressReleaseDisplay.aspx?prid=17148.

68   Ibid.

69   'Accelerating India's Growth Through Financial System Reform', *Mckinsey Quarterly*, May 2006.

70   Andy Mukherjee, 'India's Young Savers Will Prove McKinsey Wrong', 7 May 2007, www.bloomberg.com.

How Long Will It Take for India to Catch Up with China?

7

The recent optimism for accelerated economic growth in India is quite ironically a derivative of two of India's major public-policy failures. In the first flush of freedom and in an intensely nationalist phase, India chose to make Hindi its national language to phase out English. However, the non-Hindi speaking states rebelled against what was by now being described as an imposition of Hindi. In the state of Tamil Nadu, there was a full-blown secessionist movement built around this. As a part of the political accommodation that followed, this idea was quietly put on the back burner and one is not even sure if it is even on the menu now. India's recent IT successes have largely been built on the strength of its relatively low wages and English facility. It is not surprising that the IT industry is mostly centred in South India, where education in English medium is more prevalent. The other great public-policy failure, and many would still ascribe as the single major cause of all our economic woes, has been the inability to curb and stabilize the growth of population. Now many of the optimists talk about the demographic dividend. This simply means that population numbers do matter and more is actually better. And the younger it is even more beneficial.

The post-war resurgence of Japan has been the inspiration for all of Asia. Despite the near destruction of its industry, Japan's managerial and technological resources and some immediately fortuitous circumstances, such as the outbreak of the Korean War and the Cold War, created markets and alliances beneficial to its growth. But there was one other fortuitous circumstance, this was Japan's demography. Just as the USA had its baby boom after the war, Japan also had one, as Chart 7.1 below illustrates. With 35 per cent of its population below the age of 15 years in 1950, by mid-1960 Japan's baby boom was paying dividends, with the new entrants into the workforce, not only vastly increasing the ability to produce, but also with a simultaneous propensity to consume. In 2006, the thickening of the mid-section is all too evident and by 2050, Japan will be an ageing society with a decreasing and ageing population threatening growth.

In Chart 7.2 and Chart 7.4, we see a comparison of the demographic profiles of India and China from 2000 to 2050. In 2050, the thickening of China's mid-section is also all too evident. After this, China will rapidly start ageing and

Chart 7.1   Population Pyramid Summary for Japan

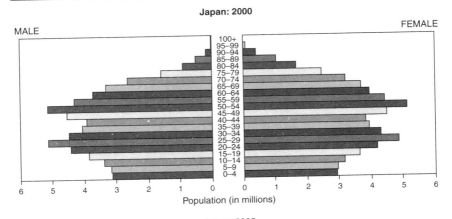

Japan: 2000

MALE

FEMALE

Population (in millions)

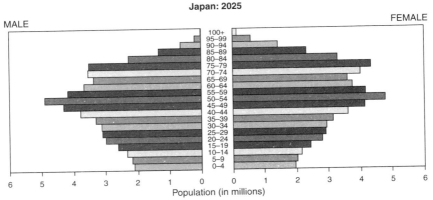

Japan: 2025

MALE

FEMALE

Population (in millions)

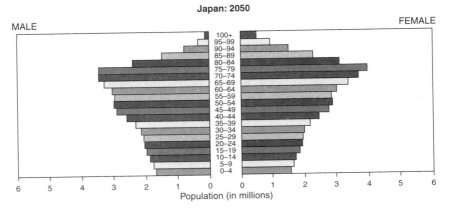

Japan: 2050

MALE

FEMALE

Population (in millions)

Source: U.S. Census Bureau, International Data Base.

Chart 7.2   Population Pyramid Summary for China

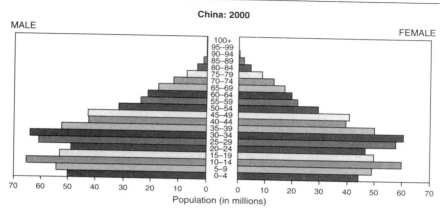

China: 2000

MALE   FEMALE

Population (in millions)

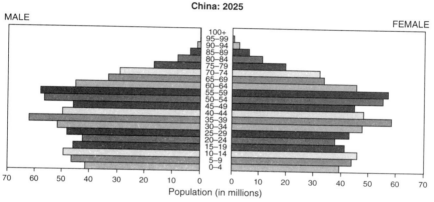

China: 2025

MALE   FEMALE

Population (in millions)

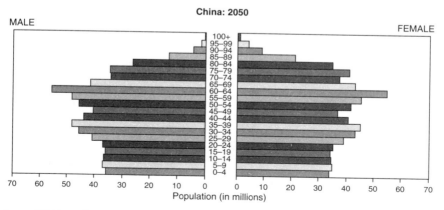

China: 2050

MALE   FEMALE

Population (in millions)

Source: U.S. Census Bureau, International Data Base.

its dependency ratio, too, will become extremely burdensome for the economy. On the other hand, India's growth phase is more sustained and it is for its leaders to exploit it to the nation's advantage. This is India's great window of opportunity. To be able to take full advantage of it, India needs to properly educate its vast population and enhance the quality of its workforce. It also needs to simultaneously upgrade and expand its infrastructure and adopt policies that speed up industrialization, and the modernization and expansion of the agricultural sector. In a politically fractious country, where the competition for power is cutthroat, this obvious road ahead is obscured by very short-term considerations. China was fortunate that it had a leader of Chairman Deng's calibre and stature, when it made its transition. In India, the critical national consensus still eludes its leadership. The national conversation still revolves around petty, parochial interests, rather than one that should normally occur in a growing power on the cusp of major transformation. Every small step towards reform and altering the status quo becomes an enervating and debilitating experience. This is the price of Indian democracy. China, by contrast, does not have a democracy but it seems to have a government that works and leads, and paradoxically, as Tarun Khanna has recently opined, more responsive to the socio-economic needs of the 'aam admi' ('common man'), than India's elites have so far demonstrated.[1]

Japan has entered the most daunting phase of its demographic transition. Savings rates will likely decline after 2005 and the old-age dependency ratio will surge by 2025. A surge in public debt compounds the problems. This decade, China's demographics are at their most favourable for economic growth. By 2025, the population will have aged a bit more, and its dependency ratio would be past its trough. But China's demographics will still look a lot better than Japan's (see Chart 7.3).

Chart 7.3   China and Japan: Mirror-image Demographics

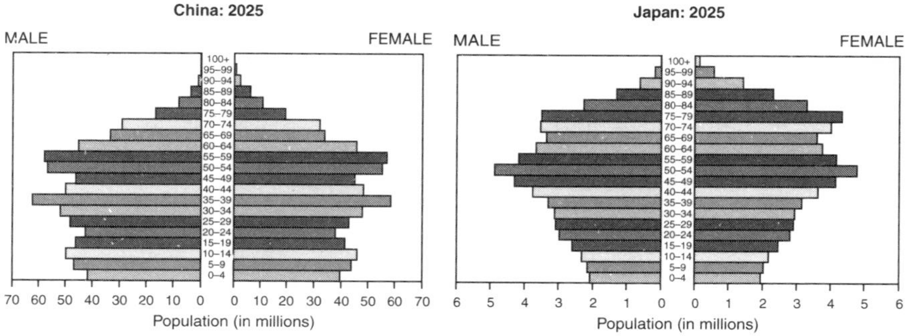

Source: U.S. Census Bureau, International Data Base.

Chart 7.4 India: Finally the Right Numbers?

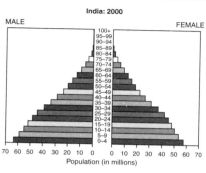

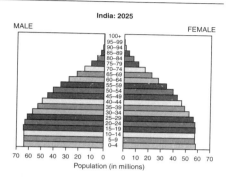

Source: U.S. Census Bureau, International Data Base.

The massive number of young people in the population today will reach the working age over the next 15–20 years. By 2025, India will have 270 million people (30 million shy of today's total US population) between the ages of 15 and 35 (see Chart 7.4). Savings rates and productive potential will be at their highest. The challenge for India is to develop a more labour-intensive growth model to take full advantage of the productive potential of these vast masses.

The challenge ahead for India is not catching up with China's growth rate, which must inevitably slow down. Can India do what China did to it in 1986? Can India come abreast with it in terms of GDP? To do that in 2025, India will need to grow at 11.6 per cent and to do that, long after most of us are gone in 2050, India must grow at 8.9 per cent every year (see Table 7.1).

Catching up with growth rates is not good enough. If that were the game, India already is doing much better than the USA, Europe and Japan! However, a study by Goldman Sachs projects that India's growth rate over the next half-century will not reach such high levels. According to this study, India's growth rates are set to peak at 6.1 per cent in 2005–10 and yet again at 2030–35 (see Table 7.5). Since 2005, India has posted a growth of about 9 per cent. Even the global slowdown has seen growth declining to 6.5 per cent. The

Table 7.1 What Will It Take for India to Catch Up with China?

India	Year	Growth Rate (%)
To catch up China by	2050	8.9
To catch up China by	2020	11.6
Average growth rate since	2000	6.2
Average growth rate in	1990s	5.6
Average growth rate in	1980s	5.6
Source: Projected on basis of current data and trends.		

Source: Goldman Sachs, CPA research

Table 7.2 Real GDP Growth Rates: Five-year
Average (Percentage Figures)

Year	India	China
2000–2005	5.3	8.0
2005–2010	6.1	7.2
2010–2015	5.9	5.9
2015–2020	5.7	5.0
2020–2025	5.7	4.6
2025–2030	5.9	4.1
2030–2035	6.1	3.9
2035–2040	6.0	3.9
2040–2045	5.6	3.5
2045–2050	5.2	2.9

Source: Goldman Sachs BRICs Model Projections

Goldman Sachs study however predicts that India's growth rate will come abreast with that of China by 2010 and overtake it by 2015.

Despite this, according to Goldman Sachs, India will not catch up with China even by 2050 (see Table 7.2). This is so, because China has a much larger GDP base than India; therefore, even smaller relative increases in income for China would mean higher absolute increases than India. It also projects that in 2050, China will be two times richer than India, in per capita terms, very similar to the present situation (see Table 7.3).

However, if India grows at a slightly better rate, and there are many indications that this optimism is warranted, then the catch-up with China doesn't seem improbable. Table 7.4 and Table 7.5 and Chart 7.5 and Chart 7.6, which

Table 7.3 Projected GDP and GDP Per Capita

Year	GDP (US$ billion)		GDP per capita (US$)	
	India	China	India	China
2000	469	1078	438	854
2005	604	1724	559	1324
2010	929	2998	804	2233
2015	1411	4754	1149	3428
2020	2104	7070	1622	4965
2025	3174	10213	2331	7051
2030	4935	14312	3473	9809
2035	7854	19605	5327	13434
2040	12367	26439	8124	18209
2045	18847	34799	12046	24192
2050	27803	44453	17366	31357

Source: Goldman Sachs BRICs Model Projections

Table 7.4 Projected GDPs for India and China till 2050 (in US$ Billion)

	India		India		India		China	
	GS Projected Growth Rate	GDP	Projected Growth Rate (+1 %)	GDP	Projected Growth Rate (+2 %)	GDP	GS Projected Growth Rate	GDP
2005*	6.1	691	7.1	691	8.1	691	7.2	1,932
2010	5.9	929	6.9	974	7.9	1,020	5.9	2,735
2015	5.7	1,238	6.7	1,360	7.7	1,492	5.0	3,642
2020	5.7	1,633	6.7	1,880	7.7	2,162	4.6	4,649
2025	5.9	2,155	6.9	2,601	7.9	3,133	4.1	5,821
2030	6.1	2,870	7.1	3,630	8.1	4,582	3.9	7,116
2035	6.0	3,859	7.0	5,116	8.0	6,764	3.9	8,617
2040	5.6	5,164	6.6	7,175	7.6	9,939	3.5	10,433
2045	5.2	6,781	6.2	9,876	7.2	14,335	2.9	12,391
2050		8,737		13,342		20,294		14,295
Average	5.8		6.8		7.8		4.6	

* Real Figures
Source:'World Development Indicators Database,' World Bank, 18 April 2006 for real figures of 2005;BRIC Report for the Projected Growth Rates, Goldman Sachs.

Table 7.5 Projected Per Capita GDPs for India and China till 2050 (in US$)

	India		India		India		China	
	GS Projected Growth Rate	per capita GDP	Projected Growth Rate (+1 %)	per capita GDP	Projected Growth Rate (+2 %)	per capita GDP	GS Projected Growth Rate	per capita GDP
2005*	6.1	626	7.1	626	8.1	626	7.2	1,468
2010	5.9	785	6.9	823	7.9	862	5.9	2,019
2015	5.7	982	6.7	1,079	7.7	1,184	5.0	2,615
2020	5.7	1,226	6.7	1,412	7.7	1,623	4.6	3,265
2025	5.9	1,544	6.9	1,864	7.9	2,245	4.1	4,038
2030	6.1	1,981	7.1	2,505	8.1	3,162	3.9	4,920
2035	6.0	2,582	7.0	3,423	8.0	4,527	3.9	5,971
2040	5.6	3,365	6.6	4,676	7.6	6,477	3.5	7,278
2045	5.2	4,325	6.2	6,300	7.2	9,144	2.9	8,745
2050		5,486		8,377		12,742		10,267
Average	5.8		6.8		7.8		4.6	

* Real Figures

Source: Calculated using data from: Population Division of the Department of Economic and Social Affairs of the United Nations Secretariat, World Population Prospects: The 2004 Revision and World Urbanization Prospects for Population Projections; 'World Development Indicators Database', World Bank, 18 April 2006 for real figures of 2005; BRIC Report for the Projected Growth Rates, Goldman Sachs.

Chart 7.5   GDP Projections for India and China till 2050

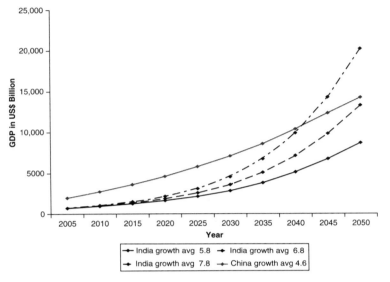

Source: Goldman Sachs BRICs Model Projections

Chart 7.6   Per Capita GDP Projections till 2050

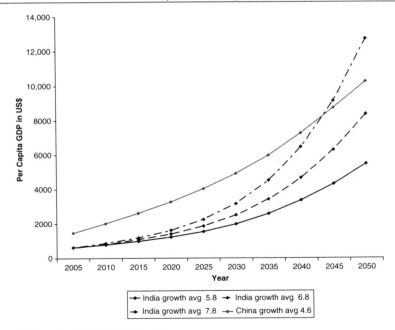

Source: Goldman Sachs BRICs Model Projections

Chart 7.7   GDP Projections till 2011

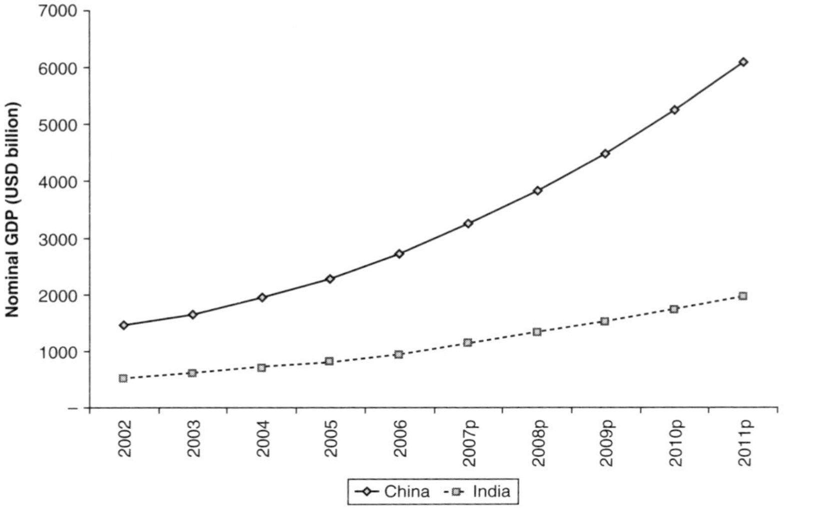

Source: The Economist Intelligence Unit, 2007

show the projected GDPs and per capita GDPs when tweaked by 1 per cent and 2 per cent respectively, indicate that India could very well catch up with China on these terms before the middle of this century. This is helped by the fact that India has a more favourable demographic situation emerging with a much larger younger population cohort, while China's population stabilizes around 2030.

Since this chapter was written, the world economy has been hit with its greatest economic crisis in a century. The crisis can be directly attributed to the cascading events in the United States, on account of its prolonged financial mismanagement, fiscal profligacy and unbridled casino capitalism. Nonetheless, we continue to remain confident of the long-term growth prospects for India and China, even if, for the next couple of years, the impact of depressed demand in the OECD world and capital scarcity will inevitably lower their GDP growth rates (see Chart 7.7).

In Chapter 8, we deal with the post-crisis world economy and reflect on the themes we have discussed so far.

NOTES

1   Tarun Khanna, *Billions of Entrepreneurs: How China and India Are Reshaping Their Futures—and Yours*, Boston, MA: Harvard Business School Press, 2008.

The Post-Crisis Challenge

8

In the last quarter of 2008, the global economy began to experience a massive economic crisis. The crisis had its immediate origins in the US financial system, which after a half-decade of excessive leverage finally came to the fore with the sub-prime crisis of August 2007. A year later it had convulsed the entire global economic system, with almost every major economy in the OECD group facing an economic recession. Alan Greenspan, former chairman of the US Federal Reserve, has described the current financial crisis as 'probably a once-in-a-century event'.

The current crisis is entirely one of American origin and a consequence of the prolonged mismanagement and under-management of both, the US economy and its financial system. When Bill Clinton handed over to George Bush in 2001, he left him with a budget surplus and a robustly growing economy. Since then the US government's finances have deteriorated sharply because of its vengeful and senseless war on Iraq and another misadventure in Afghanistan. Both wars are without UN sanction and due to USA's delusions of omnipotence. As a direct consequence, financially, matters ended up worse than before Clinton took over from the earlier Bush. In 2008 alone, the USA had a budget deficit of about US$ 455 billion.[1]

By 2008, the total debt burden of the United States had reached 350 per cent of US gross domestic product, which included household, federal and external debt, substantially higher than the 200 per cent ratio in 2000.[2] US consumption expenditure in 2008 was close to US$ 10 trillion or 70 per cent of US GDP for that year.[3] Indeed, household debt has exploded from 66 per cent of GDP in 1997 to 100 per cent of GDP in 2007. In sum, the ongoing credit crisis is the final culmination of a structural imbalance—America's quest to live beyond its means.

The USA has run a trade deficit for decades now and this grew to US$ 847 billion in 2007 and is still growing. Traditionally, it has been quite simple for the USA to bridge the ever-widening gaps because the rest of the world constantly hungered for US securities. China has over US$ 1.5 trillion in US securities and India too has over US$ 120 billion. The petrodollar economies in the Middle East weren't far behind in their hoarding of US treasuries. The simple fact of the matter is that the US dollar has a unique status as the international reserve currency—the US dollar accounts for 64 per cent of international reserves. This implies that the USA can print however many dollars it wants and can borrow endless amounts of them without feeling the consequences, that is, as long as the pyramid does not collapse.

Consequently, the USA had accumulated an external debt exceeding US$ 13.5 trillion in 2008 and this is growing by US$ 1 trillion a year since 2003.[4] If you add future envisaged outgoes to its citizens like Medicare, pensions, etc. the USA has another US$ 55 trillion due for payment. The irony is that the world and even relatively poor countries like India saw lending to the USA by buying US securities as a sound investment instead of the pyramiding scheme it had actually become. That India still sees it as a sound investment is amply reflected by the fact that there have been no withdrawals from its dollar reserves even when the rupee came under pressure due to the flight of FII capital in the aftermath of the crisis.

It is, thus, believed that the crisis was a culmination of an interrelated dynamic—over consumption in the American economy that drove demand for surplus savings in emerging markets and petrodollar economies, which were only too eager to park their surpluses in US government debt. This perpetuation of the debtor–creditor relationship, reinforced by an arrogant belief in the primacy of the US dollar as a permanent reserve currency, made US regulators and policy makers lax in their approach to this global imbalance. In fact, many of the present post-crisis interventions are premised on the dubious assumption that the US dollar will remain the world's reserve currency for all time.

The process of capital inflows into the USA were accompanied by loosening of financial oversight and risk appraisal throughout the financial system, expansion of housing mortgages to sub-prime borrowers that created an asset-price bubble in the housing market. What has been truly exceptional of this crisis has been the level of uncertainty that economists and policy makers have confronted in isolating the contaminated aspects of the financial system—the so-called toxic assets that have infiltrated the balance sheets of major financial institutions. The reason for this has been the structure of the financial markets and the role of securitization—the art of slicing up a loan and redistributing credit risk to multiple economic agents—in, paradoxically, increasing the probability of a bubble. Thus, what appeared to have been an extraordinary financial innovation, structured finance, has brought down the financial system of the industrial world.

Nonetheless, faced with a complete breakdown in the banking sector, the policy response among the industrialized countries has been a reassertion of the state as the liquidity and equity capital provider of last resort. Several 'zombie' or technically insolvent banks, which include former giants like Citigroup and Bank of America, are now being kept afloat only by regular injections of government cash. Toxic holdings in their balance sheets have severely undermined the asset positions of these banks, which now face prospects of either outright nationalizations or outright insolvency. Already, the loans, investments and guarantees made by the US government in the past year total about US$ 7,800bn, compared with a pre-crisis federal debt of about US$ 10,000bn. The estimated US federal deficit for 2009 runs as high as 12.5 per cent of GDP.[5]

The penury of Wall Street, once the epitome of American financial power, and the consequent de facto nationalization of major US financial institutions, has been aptly captured by two American economists: 'New York, once the financial capital of the world, is no longer even the financial capital of the U.S. That honor falls on Washington.'[6] The dichotomy between the real economy and wall street has been summed up by Martin Wolf:

> Over the past three decades, the debt of the US financial sector grew six times faster than nominal GDP. The consequent increases in its scale and leverage explains why, at the peak, the financial sector generated 40 per cent of US corporate profits. Something decidedly unhealthy was going on: instead of being a servant, finance had become the economy's master.[7]

Insofar as the real economy is concerned, the deflation of the housing market has had a dramatic impact on household wealth and, therefore, consumption. By end 2008, house prices had declined by about 25 per cent, but still 25 per cent above the pre-bubble level, suggesting a deeper slowdown in consumer demand in the USA remains a likely prospect.

To get a sense of the depth of the crisis in 2008, the Bank of England had estimated total losses on toxic assets at about US$ 2.8 trillion. By the end of 2008 total bank writedowns were little more than US$ 583bn.[8] At the time of writing, the US economy was contracting at an annualized rate of 5 per cent. New York University Professor Nouriel Roubini, one of the few who predicted this economic crisis, has further estimated US financial losses from the credit crisis may touch US$ 3.6 trillion, suggesting the banking system is 'effectively insolvent'.[9] Thus, we are in for a prolonged period of economic contraction, with stabilization of high-income economies, many economists opine, several years away. The International Labour Organization estimates that 51 million jobs could disappear globally by the end of 2009 taking the global unemployment rate to 7.1 per cent compared to 5.7 per cent in 2007.[10]

Returning to our theme, it would only be reasonable for the reader to question the impact of ongoing global crisis on the themes that have been advanced in this book. Bluntly put, does this crisis alter our fundamental theme—that China's economic story, especially its focus on socio-economic infrastructure such as education and healthcare, physical infrastructure such as power, water, roads, and the attendant manufacturing success offers positive lessons for India to emulate?

Before we defend our core theme, however, it is worth alluding to the impact the crisis has had on China's economic momentum, which some believed (including at moments us) was unshakable. The principal linkage by which China has been impacted has been the collapse of consumer demand in the OECD world. Thus, China's overwhelming dependence on the G-3—USA, EU and Japan account for 50 per cent of its total exports—as the principal consumer markets for its massive export machine implied it could not remain immune to a collapse in demand in these high-income economies. Indeed, in Chapter 5, we had shown that East Asian geo-economic trends were intrinsically linked to extra-regional demand in the West.

Chart 8.1   China's Economic Performance

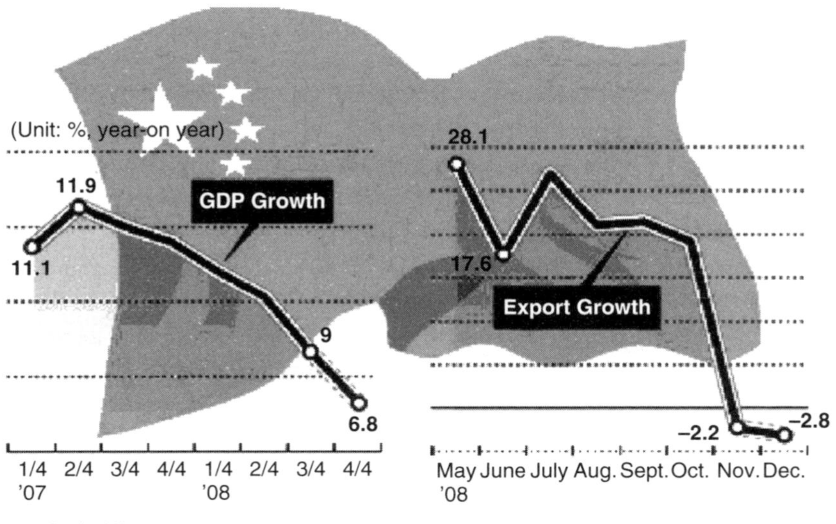

Source: Bank of Korea

Three of East Asia's powerhouse economies—China, Japan and South Korea—faced with falling demand for their exports are experiencing a painful slowdown of their own. China's latest Q4 GDP numbers for 2008 reveal it is growing at its slowest pace in the last seven years. China said its economy expanded by 6.8 per cent in the fourth quarter compared to the same period the year before. Japanese exports plunged a record 35 per cent in December 2008. South Korea said its economy shrank by 3.4 per cent in the last quarter of 2008. China's exports slumped last month at their fastest pace in a decade, with their value declining by 2.8 per cent year-on-year, the worst performance since April 1999, while its imports plummeted by 21.3 per cent.[11]

Clearly, China with its interdependent economic relationship with America is now facing the brunt of the readjustment process—as US over absorption is no longer feasible in the prevailing phase of a financial implosion, and no other economies even collectively can assume the consumption burden of America, Chinese overproduction must inevitably pull back as well. This would suggest a structural lowering of the trend growth rate in China. In this process of rebalancing growth, China's consumption spending ratio of 36 per cent of GDP will need to rise to sustain the growth of aggregate demand.

The state-backed Chinese Academy of Social Sciences said the unemployment rate including migrant workers, who constitute the export-related workforce, may be higher than 9.4 per cent in 2009, the highest in 30 years.[12] Already, a government survey carried out in 15 Chinese provinces suggests around 20 million workers or 15 per cent of the total migrant labour pool is now unemployed.[13]

In retrospect, China's export-led development process and the manufacturing scale that China brought to the global trading system always implied the existence of reciprocal demand centres. A breakdown in this symbiotic relationship has now occurred with its epicenter in the USA. Whether China can sustain its double-digit-growth momentum will be determined by the emergence of new deficit centres, albeit smaller in scale than the USA, and a parallel increase in Chinese internal demand.

It is worth pointing out that China's policy instruments, especially healthy fiscal balances and possession of huge foreign exchange reserves provide Beijing's planners with sufficient instruments to avoid a deep recession. China has already introduced a US$ 586bn stimulus package[14], cut interest rates five times since September 2008, and lowered taxes. It should be recalled that China's counter-cyclical fiscal policies helped stimulate the economy in the aftermath of the Asian Financial Crisis. Back then, the budget deficit increased from 0.7 per cent of GDP in 1998 to 2.6 per cent of GDP in 2000.[15] In Chapter 6, we had noted that China's approach to economic globalization has been calibrated with a parallel expansion of state presence in the major industrial sectors. In the ongoing crisis, Beijing's state-owned sector will be tested as it seeks to stabilize the economy, and such a 'technocratic ideology', as economist Huang Yasheng calls it or 'state capitalism' as others refer to it, is likely to only get more pronounced in the years ahead.[16]

China and India, both temporarily chastened, will hereon need to introspect on their current approach to economic development and more honestly assess the formidable path to industrialization that lies ahead. With globalization, as we have come to recognize, no longer an inevitable course for the international political economy, both these Asian powers will need to conceive a development template less dependent on the Western industrialized world.

It must be pointed out that if India has avoided the most extreme effects of the global recession it is, ironically, because it failed to broaden the structure of its economy by focusing on industrialization. This as we noted during the course of the book has been largely a structural failure to increase the contribution of manufacturing and merchandize trade as a proportion of GDP. Thus, an overdependence on services has enabled India to remain *relatively* insulated from the slowdown that has punished the export-oriented manufacturing industries of its northern neighbour and almost the entire East Asian region.[17] This, however, can hardly be any consolation for India's economic managers, and should certainly not become an excuse for policy inaction. Nonetheless, India's export sector, which accounts for 22 per cent of GDP and employs 150 million workers (the second largest employer after agriculture) is likely to lose 10 million jobs by March 2009, according to estimates from the Federation of Indian Export Organisations trade group.[18]

It must be reiterated that services by itself cannot rejuvenate and transform India into a sustainable economic force. Throughout history, industrialization has been and will continue to be the only sustainable development path, especially of a population the size of India's and the composition and literacy levels of its workforce. To reallocate the 60 per cent of India that barely sustains its less-than-modest livelihood on an agrarian sector growing at an average rate of 2 per cent for the past decade, a focus on manufacturing is imperative. In this context, it should be recalled that China's first decade of reform was driven largely by the agricultural sector, and the ensuing linkages that it created for rural industries to flourish.

The principal failure of India's economic planners has been their dismal record in shaping the conditions to leverage India's comparative advantage— its huge pool of unskilled workforce—in the development template. With approximately 14 million Indians, entirely unskilled, entering the labour force each year, the challenge of job creation can hardly be overstated. Hence our focus during the course of this book to point out the limits of skill-based development (service sector growth) for India.

And for manufacturing, especially for achieving scale in labour-intensive sectors, a pan-Indian provision of core infrastructure services is essential. Even today, for every US$ 1 that India spends on infrastructure, China spends US$ 7. In 2007, India added 7,000 MW to its power capacity; China added 100,000 MW. A recent study of input–output structure identified 10 vital sectors in the Indian economy based on growth impacts on GDP of efficiency improvements in these sectors. These sectors include electricity, water/gas supply, transport services, railway transport services, coal and lignite, etc. The study found that India's growth rate is at least as sensitive to these sectors as it was prior to the 1991 reforms.[19] More generally, supply-side bottlenecks continue to constrain Indian industry.

India's financial globalization or integration to Western capital markets, however, was relatively high preceding the crisis. As much of the speculative or 'hot money' that had parked itself in India's capital markets got sucked out and returned to the safety of more durable currencies, India Inc. has taken a beating. Much of India's private sector credit expansion aside from internal accruals emanated from external borrowing and infusion of foreign equity capital. At end-2008, commercial borrowings accounted for 28 per cent (or US$ 66 billion) of India's total external debt. Now with the liquidity boom that fuelled much of global and India's growth for the past five years finally over, the credit to sustain India's growth rates and finance massive infrastructure projects (estimated at US$ 500 billion until 2012) will be a formidable policy challenge. Greater mobilization of domestic savings will be imperative to finance the investment plans for the public and private sectors in India. In this regard, another paradox of India's growth story over the recent years must be highlighted. Despite being a capital scarce country, India has been a net capital exporter in recent years. In 2006–07, India's gross exports of FDI were a whopping 12 per cent of GDP, and much of this was destined for the OECD countries.[20]

It might also be noted that the intellectual response of many commentators in India has been disappointing. Instead of seeking to investigate the causes of and drawing the right lessons of the current Western crisis, many are simply hoping for a renewal of the (unsustainable) economic systems of the industrialized world. But the status-quo ante is unlikely to be restored. Some in India appear more eager for the Sensex, which lost 60 per cent of its value in 2008, to recover the abnormal peaks of the past few years!

At both a policy-relevant and ideological level, if there is one principal lesson from the international economic crisis it is arguably, that there is a need for more not less *state* to confront the opportunities and challenges of globalization. In fact, the Western Anglo-Saxon economic model of unfettered free-market capitalism, the principal benchmark for economic management for many emerging economies has turned on itself, and according to many Western economists, has lost its credibility as the utopian economic model it could once claim to be.

It is important here to note that India's memory of its discredited socio-economic model of the pre-reform era and the crony-capitalist state that accompanied it should not become an obstacle for more enlightened governance and regulation, an unavoidable necessity of the globalized era, and indeed a prerequisite to fulfilling the objective of inclusive, pan-Indian growth.

A failure here would involve facing the dangerous risk of alienating the majority of rural India, and destabilization or even complete breakdown in the nation-building and development process. Economic interdependence by definition precludes the prospect of insulation in turbulent times; if there is one global lesson that this crisis brings home, it is that the state is the only and final arbiter of economic security. Thus, for the growth and technological benefits of globalization to be wholly exploited and sensibly managed, it must be accompanied by a renewal of the state itself.

CONCLUSION

For the first time since the early 1800s, India along with China and other non-European nations are on the cusp of achieving a dignified position in the international political economy. India and China are clearly set to emerge as two important economic centres. They are also neighbours, who will increasingly compete for resources, markets and influence. It is not inevitable that India and China will again become mortal enemies. The likelihood of armed conflict is now much reduced with both countries acquiring a greater stake in the international political economy. Yet, the nature of the international anarchic system will ensure that both countries will be competitors. But to ensure that this does not turn into yet another Cold War, India must not only ensure that the absolute economic gap with China is narrowed but that it implements the structural transformation of its growth model to emerge as a large-scale manufacturing economy. This process will inevitably involve the Indian state to implement active and enlightened state policies that shape the structure of a number of vital industries in the decades to come. The state will also need to reassert itself in ensuring an efficient provision of 'core public goods'— both physical infrastructure, such as energy, water supply, roads, ports and socio-economic infrastructure, such as education and healthcare. Suffice it to say, the free-market euphoria among some of India's economists and policy managers as the dominant template for India's economic transition is empirically unjustified as demonstrated by the Chinese (or larger East Asian) experience and ill-suited for India's socio-economic and strategic situation. The present economic turmoil only underscores the need for a responsible role for the state in the management of the economic system.

Clearly, India's political leadership has its job cut out. But are they up to it?

NOTES

1   US Congressional Budget Office (www.cbo.gov/).

2   Martin Wolf, 'Seeds of Its Own Destruction', *Financial Times*, 8 March 2009.

3   US Bureau of Economic Analysis (www.bea.gov/).

4   US Treasury Department Data (www.ustreas.gov/).

5   Niall Ferguson, 'The Age of Obligation', *Financial Times*, 19 Dec 2008.

6   Ian Bremmer and Nouriel Roubini, 'Expect the World Economy to Suffer Through 2009', *The Wall Street Journal*, 23 Jan 2009.

7   Martin Wolf, 'Why Dealing with the Huge Debt Overhang Is So Hard', *Financial Times*, 27 January 2009.

8   Niall Ferguson, 'An Imaginary Retrospective of 2009', *Financial Times*, 15 Dec 2009.

9   Henry Meyer and Ayesha Daya, 'Roubini Predicts U.S. Losses May Reach $3.6 Trillion', www.bloomberg.com, 20 Jan 2009.

10 'Global Job Losses "Could Hit 51m"', BBC News, http://news.bbc.co.uk, 28 January 2009.

11 Kim Jae-Kyoung, 'Korea Braces for China Shock', www.koreatimes.co.kr, 27 January 2009.

12 Li Yanping, 'China Faces Worst Unemployment in Decades as Slowdown Deepens', www.bloomberg.com, 20 January 2009.

13 Chris Hogg, 'Chinese Migrant Job Losses Mount', http://news.bbc.co.uk, 2 February 2009.

14 Beijing has announced a two-year-spending programme on infrastructure and social welfare, though has not indicated how much of this was not already planned.

15 *China Quarterly Update*, The World Bank, December 2008.

16   Jamil Anderlini, 'China's State Sector Urged to Boost Economy', *Financial Times*, 26 December 2008.

17   To be sure, the IT services sector and its overwhelming dependence on Western markets have inevitably impacted its growth prospects.

18   Cherian Thomas, 'India Exports Fell in December for 3rd Straight Month', www.bloomberg.com, 2 February 2009.

19   Nirvikar Singh, 'The Ten Sectors that Need a Boost', *Financial Express*, 12 December 2006.

20   Arvind Subramanian, 'Precocious India', *Business Standard*, 14 August 2007.

APPENDIX

Policy Note

The Vital Role for Anti-Trust in India

The role of anti-trust is perhaps one of the most powerful policy instruments available to the state in a market economy. Consistent with our theme of a strategic economic policy for India—antitrust policy assumes critical salience, especially when the often competing policy goals of preserving consumer welfare (preventing abuse of dominant market power) at home clash with the strategic objective of encouraging large globally relevant corporations to thrive.

I.

Historical Backdrop: The overwhelming presence of the government (public-sector units—PSUs) in several sectors of the economy meant that independent regulators were rarely required since the state controlled high market shares in several industries. Conflicts of interest also implied the futility of such an exercise in the absence of credible private-sector participation. Yet, in 1964, two large business houses accounted for 11 per cent of all private corporate assets in India other than banking and comprised 30 per cent of the total assets of the 75 major Indian firms.[1] To ameliorate this relatively high concentration of power in India, the Monopolies and Restrictive Trade Practices (MRTP) Act was enacted in 1969. However, the prevalent parallel industrial policies of the time restricted competition. All the process attributes of competition such as entry, price, scale, location, etc. were regulated. Paradoxically then, the MRTP Act was enacted to address competition concerns that stemmed from the *license raj*! Suffice it to say it had minimal influence on market development—a pre-requisite for competition.

The Post-1991 Scenario:

- Several sectors were opened to private participation. Hence, circumstances have altered the rationale for minimal or rhetorical regulation.

- Increased competition in several industries have shifted the onus back to the state to ensure a competitive environment prevails—i.e., prevent collusion, cartels, private monopolies—and balancing this mandate with the positive incentives of innovation (intellectual property issues), R&D, etc.

- An additional rationale for enhanced antitrust regulation is that the level of import penetration into several deregulated sectors has been low. Since import liberalization is occurring gradually, regulators need to assume a larger responsibility to ensure a competitive environment prevails.[2] When coupled with India's inefficient port infrastructure and physical connectivity to major industrial locations, the landed price of imports is in many instances not competitive with big domestic business houses.

- Similarly, a liberalized FDI regime would theoretically serve as a competition policy tool. Again, India's case suggests that this has had a limited influence on competition, at least until very recently.

- While the Government's multiple roles as social and economic manager, owner of state assets, business operator have evolved, the fundamental features have endured—a strong presence in several industrial and infrastructure sectors.

- The Competition Act of 2002 and the creation of the Competition Commission.[3] The Commission, however, largely has an advisory role and its autonomy is severely impaired by a number of institutional constraints.

Which Model to Adopt? The liberal US antitrust model has an implicit mandate to advance innovation and relies primarily on the market to advance and sustain competition and efficiency. For instance, fewer M&As are rejected in the US compared to Europe. The EU on the other hand has forged a far more aggressive competition policy that has a broader mandate whose 'stakeholders' go beyond the specific industry's customers and competitors to achieve other ends.[4] Research has indicated that the two models reflect the socio-economic and political systems in which they operate and an optimal model for one may not be appropriate for the other.[5]

Sequencing of Reforms: Studies have shown that liberalization measures are prone to fail unless preceded (or accompanied) by the creation of appropriate regulatory frameworks. Russian experience of the 1990s is a prime example. This is a fundamental reason to defer Indian privatization. On the other hand, proponents have advocated a 'shock therapy' approach involving the swift divestiture of the state's economic holdings. The logic is that this rapid deregulation would best stimulate the development of market processes and create a constituency for further regulatory reforms. This characterizes to some extent the Indian experiment in the early 1990s where deregulated sectors drove further regulation. The downside, however, that economists such as Stiglitz have alluded to is far more dangerous. Without adequate attention, the divestment of assets may simply reincarnate obdurate state monopolies as durable privately held monopolies.[6] The case of Reliance Group where its acquisition of IPCL, a PSU, increased its market share to ˜90% in the petrochemical industry exemplifies this point.

II. Competition Intensity in India's Manufacturing Industry:
The Post-Reform Period

This section examines the empirical evidence in terms of the pattern of market concentration in select manufacturing sectors.[7] The Herfindhal-Hirshchman Index (HH Index) is employed as a measure of market power. The HHI of a market is calculated by summing the squares of the percentage market shares held by the respective firms. The index declines with increasing number of firms. A total monopoly would imply an HH index of 10,000 (square of 100). According to the US Department of Justice's *1992 Horizontal Merger Guidelines*, the agency regards a market in which the post-merger HHI is below 1000 as 'unconcentrated,' between 1000 and 1800 as 'moderately concentrated,' and above 1800 as 'highly concentrated' (see Table A.1, Chart A.1 and Table A.2).

Table A.1   Trend in HH Index in Select Industries

Industry	1994	2005	Dominant Company	Market Share
Copper & Copper Products	780	4,867	Sterlite Industries	68%
Polyster Staple Fibre (PSF)	1,800	8,140	Reliance Industries	90%
Viscose Staple Fibre (VSF)	7,700	10,000	Grasim Industries	100%
Storage Batteries	2,900	5,199	Exide Industries	69%
Television Picture Tubes	1,800	5,536	Samtel Color	71%

Source: Computed from 'Market Size and Shares' in Centre for Monitoring Indian Economy (CMIE) Database

Chart A.1   Trend in HH Index in Select Industries

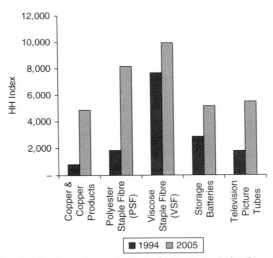

Source: Computed from 'Market Size and Shares' in Centre for Monitoring Indian Economy (CMIE) Database

Table A.2   Merger Behaviour of MRTP Companies—Pre- and Post-1991 Amendments

	1986–1991	1992–1997
% of mergers companies belong to the same business group	17% (13 out of 77)	63% (60 out of 96)
% of mergers companies belong to the same product category	38% (22 out of 58)	53% (48 out of 90)

Source: *See footnote 8*

Observations:

- It is clear that private firms have assumed dominant positions in several industries since the trade and industrial liberalization in the early 1990s.

- The observed range of concentration levels may be high relative to developed economies. For instance, in the US, for a large number of manufacturing industries the

HH index is reported to be less than 1000. This feature can be explained by India's relative smaller market size of industry (& GDP), as many industries do not have the depth to accommodate many efficient firms.

- Low import penetration in many industries could also account for high concentration levels.

- Weak M&A guidelines, at least from a competition perspective, also account for this trend. Additionally, the majority of mergers in the post-1991 period have come through horizontal combinations.

- From an antitrust perspective, the critical challenge is to distinguish between cases where market dominance has been attained through superior efficiency, from those that were achieved by predatory conduct.

III.

The ambiguities and complexities of antitrust law stem from several intersecting, but often competing, interests and objectives. The purpose of this brief is to offer a concise analysis of the broad issues and provide a snapshot of global trends that may be of interest to policy planners. It is clear that a competition policy system, respecting specific industry dynamics must be in place for a transition economy such as India to benefit from further deregulation. To be sure, all public policy tools must be synchronized to get results.[8] India's advantage over other transition economies lies in the fact that it already has a mature institutional framework and a credible judicial system that respects property rights. The challenge is coordinating these often disparate bodies toward creating a regulatory environment suited to market development.

Policy Recommendations:

I. **Which model[9]?:** At the outset of this paper, the two principal Western antitrust models were briefly evaluated. On balance, it might be a proper choice for Indian competition policy to concentrate on its traditional core business (i.e. maintenance of competition) and not attempt to manage externalities in an ineffective way. Additionally, the political economy of India's development suggests that independent regulation, though imperfect, provides better safeguards against the excesses of a state highly penetrated by corporate actors.[10] On the whole, it must be noted that the EU approach that evaluates long-term harm to a competitive landscape is more beneficial that the USA's near-term approach.

II. **Re-regulation of 'deregulated' sectors:** The new Competition Act (2002) that endeavours to advance efficiency rather than preventing monopolies is a welcome step. Yet, sectors where the government is no longer a major player would require astute regulation and would be more susceptible to regulatory capture or abuse by dominant firms. As stated earlier, privatization by itself is not a 'magic bullet'. The required competitive discipline after deregulation seldom occurs if unaided by policy tools. Hence, it must be preceded or accompanied by sound regulation if welfare-reducing outcomes are to be avoided.

III. **M&As:** As part of 1991 amendments, the MRTP Act was diluted by removing provisions on mergers and acquisitions to allow for inorganic growth.[11] Consequently, there was no M&A regulation from a competition perspective. While the new Competition Act does have provisions for monitoring combinations, these are very narrow and have a very high threshold with the result that many M&As would escape its scrutiny. Recent indications suggest the government is proposing to extend its oversight.[12]

IV. **Public sector units (PSUs):** The state continues to play a major role in industries such as the telecommunications, oil and gas, power, water, steel, airlines, and shipping. In these sectors, although the concentration of private participation varies, the lack of an 'arm's length' between the regulator and the relevant PSU poses additional issues. While the PSU's presence ensures a counterbalance in case the regulator fails to enforce private competition, it injects another variable into the regulator's calculus. TRAI is an excellent example of Indian regulator that reconciled its mandate to promote competition, while preserving the viability and interests of the two major PSUs (BSNL, MTNL).

V. **Antitrust and global competition:** The recent trend of large conglomerates in global supply chains has implications for Indian policy makers as they prepare to instill dynamic antitrust regulation in (privatized) deregulated sectors.[13] The point here is that since major industries globally are dominated by few giant firms, national anti-trust authorities now have an additional variable in their already overcrowded portfolios—the imperative to enable domestic firms to gain the size by which they can compete overseas. Of course, the flipside is stifling domestic competition. The role of antitrust, therefore, plays a critical role in such an exercise that reconciles the internal need for market development (and competition) with the external need to allow indigenous, large, global, competitive corporations to emerge.

VI. **A Competition Policy for India's Knowledge Economy:** Until now, the onus of regulating the IT economy has fallen on the West. This was because 'outsourcing' and 'offshoring' activities that Indian software companies exported were at the low-end of the value chain (i.e. call centre services, functional support, data storage, etc.). But with Indian software companies moving up the value chain and focusing more on R&D and creating new 'products', the onus will shift back to local regulators to enforce competition and advance innovation. In the digital economy, competition revolves around the efforts to maintain the legal protection afforded by Intellectual Property (IP) law. Effective antitrust regulation must, therefore, be based on new integrative approaches that explicitly take into account the interaction between IP rights and competition policy.[14]

NOTES

1   Narayana Rao Rampilla, 'A Developing Judicial Perspective to India's Monopolies and Restrictive Trade Practices Act of 1969', *Antitrust Bulletin*, Vol. 34, Iss. 3, (New York: Fall 1989), p. 655, 28 pgs.

2   This point has another public policy dimension here. Insofar as there is a need to build a larger domestic industrial base to 'correct' the lop-sided service sector contribution to GDP, there is a clear logic in pacing import liberalization in atleast the non-intermediate manufacturing sector.

3   The 2002 Act is now part of Indian jurisprudence. Through a Government notification of 31st March 2003, certain sections of the new Act are now in force. However, until the full commission is appointed and remaining provisions of the new law are introduced, the old MRTP commission will continue to function.

4   The 'new' horizontal agreements approach in the EU: An 'economic' assessment, Hans Maks, Intereconomics, Hamburg, Jan/Feb 2002, Vol.37, Issue 1; pg. 28, 8 pgs; Carlin, W., Fries, S., Schaffer, M.E. and Seabright, P. (2001) Competition and Enterprise Performance in Transition Economies: Evidences from a Cross-country Survey, CEPR Discussion Paper No. 2840.

Thomas E. Kauper, Merger control in the United States and the European Union: Some observations, St. Johns Law Review; Spring 2000; 74; 2.

Also see the Financial Times for a recent survey of across the board revival of antitrust activity and concern of excessive concentration in a number of industries.

5   'Are efficient antitrust rules always optimal?', Brett H McDonnell, Daniel A Farber, Antitrust Bulletin, New York: Fall 2003, Vol.48, Iss. 3; pg. 807, 29 pgs; US-EU in a Comparative Perspective:

Time Horizons
* US – merger review process requires near-term foreseeable adverse effect
* EC – looks to long-term speculative harm

Dominance – necessarily harmful to competition?
* US – no, if consumers are not marginalized and if it induces innovation and efficiency
* EU – yes, if it squeezes competitors out of the market

Pro-competitor or Pro-consumer?
* US – takes into consideration competitor complaints but emphasis on consumer welfare
* EU - likely to consider and be influenced by views of competitors reactions

6   Joseph Stiglitz, 'Knowledge for Development: Economic Science, Economic Policy, and Economic Advise', in Annual World Bank Conference on Development Economics (1998).

7   The criterion used to select industries is that they have multiple applications or are intermediate products that form a critical part of an industrial value chain.

8   Rakesh Basant & Sebastian Morris, 'Competition Policy in India: Issues for a Globalizing Economy', *Economic and Political Weekly*, 29 July 2000.

9   For a recent and extensive analysis on antitrust issues in India see, Pradeep S Mehta (edited), A Functional Competition Policy for India, Published by Academic Foundation & CUTS, 2006.

10   For an excellent case study see, Rahul Mukherji, 'Managing Competition: Politics and the Building of Independent Regulatory Institutions', India Review, Vol. 2, No. 4, October 2004.

11   After it enacted in 1969, the MRTP underwent a number of amendments, most notably in 1984 and 1991. The 1991 amendment removed all pre-entry restrictions on M&As.

12   'India Plans New Panel to Look into Corporate M&As', *Reuters*, 29 August 2007.

13   Barry Lynn, 'Wake Up to the Old-fashioned Power of the New Oligopolies', *Financial Times*, 15 February 2006. For a more extensive elaboration of Barry Lynn's ideas see his book, End of the Line: The Rise and Coming Fall of the Global Corporation, 2005 where the author empirically shows the radical re-organization from highly vertically-integrated to transnational global production networks is the result of globalization but also the source of (US) economic insecurity. The impetus for this originally stemmed from relaxed US antitrust in the 1990s.

14   Gary Minda, 'Antitrust Regulability and the New Digital Economy: A Proposal for Integrating 'Hard' and 'Soft' Regulation', *Antitrust Bulletin*, Vol. 46, Iss. 3; (New York: Fall 2001) p. 439, 73 pgs.

BIBLIOGRAPHY

BOOKS

Archarya, Shankar, *Can India Grow Without Bharat?* (New Delhi: Academic Foundation, 2007).

Breslin, Shaun, *China and the Global Political Economy* (New York: Palgrave Macmillan, 2007).

Chang, Ha-Joon, *Globalisation, Economic Development and the Role of the State* (London: Zed Books, 2003).

Chang, Ha-Joon, *Kicking Away the Ladder: Development Strategy in Historical Perspective* (London: Anthem Press, 2003).

Corden, W. Max, *Too Sensational: On the Choice of Exchange Rate Regimes* (Cambridge, Massachusetts: MIT Press, 2002).

Dahlman, Carl and Anuja Utz, *India and the Knowledge Economy: Leveraging Strengths and Opportunities* (Washington, DC: World Bank, July 2005).

Fu, J., *Institutions and Investments: Foreign Direct Investment in China During an Era of Reforms* (Ann Arbor: University of Michigan Press, 2000).

Huang, Yasheng, *Selling China: Foreign Direct Investment During the Reform Era* (New York: Cambridge University Press, 2003).

Jha, Prem Shankar, *The Perilous Road to the Market—The Political Economy of Reform in Russia, India, and China* (London: Pluto Press, 2002).

Khanna, Tarun, *Billions of Entrepreneurs: How China and India Are Reshaping Their Futures—and Yours* (Cambridge, Massachusetts: Harvard Business School Press, 2008).

Lardy, Nicholas, *Integrating China into the Global Economy* (Washington, D.C.: Brookings Institution Press, 2002).

Lynn, Barry, *End of the Line: The Rise and Coming Fall of the Global Corporation*, (New York: Doubleday Books, 2005).

Maddison, Angus, *The World Economy: A Millennial Perspective* (OECD Development Centre Studies, 2001).

Maddison, Angus, *World Population, GDP and Per Capita GDP, 1-2003 AD*, (Groningen: University of Groningen, November 2006).

McKenney, K. I., *An Assessment of China's Special Economic Zones* (Washington, D.C.: Fort McNair, 1993).

Riedel, James, Jing Jin, and Jian Gao, *How China Grows: Investment, Finanace and Reform* (New Jersey: Princeton University Press, 2007).

Sasuga, Katsuhiro, *Microregionalism and Governance in East Asia* (London; New York: Routledge, 2004).

Sinha, Aseema, 'Ideas, Interests, and Institutions in Policy Change: A Comparison of West Bengal and Gujarat' in Rob Jenkins (edited), *Regional Reflections Comparing Politics across India's States* (New Delhi: Oxford University Press, 2004).

ECONOMIC PAPERS

'Accelerating India's Growth Through Financial System Reform', Mckinsey Global Institute, May 2006.

Anderson, Jonathan, 'Solving China's Rebalancing Puzzle', *Finance and Development*, IMF, Volume 44, Number 3, September 2007.

Ando, Mitsuyo (Hitotsubashi University), and Fukinari Kimura (Keio University), 'Fragmentation in East Asia: Further Evidence', January 2007.

Ando, Mitsuyo, and Fukinari Kimura, 'The Formation of International Production and Distribution Networks in East Asia', NBER Working Paper 10167, National Bureau of Economic Research, Cambridge, MA, 2003.

Athukorala, Prema-chandra, The Rise of China and East Asian Export Performance: Is the Crowding-out Fear Warranted?, Working Paper No. 2007/10, Australian National University, September 2007.

Athukorala, Prema-chandra, 'Multinational Production Networks and the New Geo-Economic Division of Labour in the Pacific Rim', Australian National University, 2006.

Bai, Chong-En, Chang-Tai Hsieh, and Yingyi Qian, 'The Return to Capital in China', NBER Working Paper No. 12755, December 2006.

Banga, Rashmi and B. N. Goldar, 'Contribution of Services to Output Growth Productivity in Indian Manufacturing: Pre and Post Reform', *ICRIER Working paper* No. 139, 2004.

Barnett, Steven and Ray Brooks, 'What's Driving Investment in China?', IMF Working Paper, November 2006.

Bhaskaran, 'China as Potential Superpower: Regional Responses', Deutsche Bank Research Report, 2003.

Bosworth, Barry, Susan M. Collins, Arvind Virmani, 'Sources of Growth in the Indian Economy', NBER Working Paper 12901, February 2007.

Carlin, W., Fries, S., Schaffer, M. E. and Seabright, P., 'Competition and Enterprise Performance in Transition Economies: Evidences from a Cross-country Survey', CEPR Discussion Paper No. 2840, 2001.

Corden, W. Max, 'Too Sensational: On the Choice of Exchange Rate Regimes' (MIT Press, 2002), pp. 42, 219–223.

Eichengreen, Barry and Hui Tong, 'Is China's FDI Coming at the Expense of Other Countries?', NBER Working Papers 11335, MA, 2005.

Gaulier, Lemoine & Kesenci, 'China's Emergence and the Reorganization of Trade Flows in Asia', CEPII, Working Paper, March 2006.

Gordon, James, and Poonam Gupta, 'Understanding India's Services Revolution', IMF Working Paper WP/04/171, September (2004).

Haddad, Mona, 'Trade Integration in East Asia: The Role of China and Production Networks', World Bank Policy Research Working Paper No. 4160, 1 March 2007.

Hansda, Sanjay K., 'Sustainability of Services-led Growth: An Input-Output Analysis of Indian Economy', RBI Occasional Working Paper, Vol. 22, No. 1, 2 and 3, 2001.

Jaimovich, Nir and Henry Siu, 'The Young, the Old, and the Restless: Demographics and Business Cycle Volatility', February 2007.

Jen, Stephen, 'How Big Could Sovereign Wealth Funds Be by 2015?', Morgan Stanley Research: Economics, 3 May 2007.

Jen, Stephen, 'Sovereign Wealth Funds and Official FX Reserves', Morgan Stanley Research: Economics, 14 September 2006.

Kapur, Devesh and Pratap Bhanu Mehta, 'Indian Higher Education Reform: From Half-Baked Socialism to Half-Baked Capitalism', CID Working Paper No. 108, September 2004.

Kochhar, K., Kumar U., Rajan R., Subramanian A., and Tokatlidis I., 'India's Pattern of Development: What Happened, What Follows', IMF Working Paper, January 2006.

Kokko, Ari, 'Export-Led Growth In East Asia: Lessons For Europe's Transition Economies', Stockholm School of Economics, Working Paper no. 142, 2002.

Kuijs, Louis, 'Investment and Saving in China', World Bank Policy Research Working Paper 3633, June 2005.

Kuijs, Louis and Kim, Song-Yi, 'Raw Material Prices, Wages, and Profitability in China Industry: How Was Profitability Maintained when Input Prices and Wages Increased So Fast?', World Bank China Research Paper No. 8, October 2007.

Leadbeater, Charles and Wilsdon, James, 'How Asian Innovation Can Benefit Us All', *Atlas of Ideas: Mapping the New Geography of Science*, Demos, January 2007.

Liang, Hong, 'China's Investment Strength is Sustainable', Global Economics Paper No: 146, Goldman Sachs, 3 October 2006.

Maks, Hans, 'The "New" Horizontal Agreements Approach in the EU: An "Economic" Assessment, Intereconomics', Hamburg, Jan/Feb 2002, Vol.37, Issue 1; pg. 28, 8 pgs.

Mishra, Deepak, 'Can India Attain the East Asian Growth with South Asian Saving Rate?', World Bank, July 2006 First Draft.

Naughton, Barry, 'China's Emergence and Prospects as a Trading Nation', Economic Studies Program, Volume 27, 1996.

National Commission for Enterprises in the Unorganised Sector (NCEUS), Report on Conditions of Work and Promotion of Livelihood in the Unorganised Sector, 2007. (Access report at: http://nceus.gov.in/Condition_of_workers_sep_2007.pdf).

Nikomborirak, Deunden, A Comparative Study of the Role of the Service Sector in the Economic Development of China And India (Revised report), Thailand Development Research Institute, 19 June 2006.

Papola, T. S., 'Emerging Structure of India Economy: Implications of growing Inter-Sectoral Imbalances', Presidential Address, at the 88th Conference of Indian Economic Association, Andhara University, Vishakhapatram, 2005.

Rahardja, Sjamsu, 'Big Dragon, Little Dragons: China's Challenge to the Machinery Exports of Southeast Asia', Policy Research Working Paper 4297, The World Bank East Asia and Pacific Region Financial and Private Sector Unit, August 2007.

Rodrik, Dani, 'What's So Special about China's Exports?', NBER Working Paper 11947, National Bureau of Economic Research, Cambridge, MA, 2006.

Singh Nirvikar, 'Services-Led Industrialization in India: Prospects and Challenges', Working Paper No. 290, Stanford Center for International Development, August 2006, updated November 2006.

Srinivasan, T. N., 'Comments on From "Hindu Growth" to Productivity Surge: The Mystery of the Indian Growth Transition', IMF Staff Papers, September 2005, Vol. 52, No. 2.

Srinivasan, T. N., 'China, India and the World Economy', Working Paper No. 286, July 2006.

Stiglitz, Joseph, 'Knowledge for Development: Economic Science, Economic Policy, and Economic Advice', Annual World Bank Conference on Development Economics, 1998.

'The Atlas of Ideas: Mapping the New Geography of Science', DEMOS, 2007.

Wilson, Dominic and Roopa Purushothaman, 'Dreaming with the BRICs: The Path to 2050', Global Economics Paper No. 99, Goldman Sachs, New York, 1 October 2003.

'World Investment Prospects to 2011: Foreign Direct Investment and the Challenge of Political Risk', Economist Intelligence Unit (www.eiu.com), 2007.

Wu, Friedrich, Poa Tiong Siaw, Yeo Han Sia and Puah Kok Keong, 'Foreign Direct Investments to China and Southeast Asia: Has Asean Been Losing Out?' Economic Survey of Singapore.

Xiao, 'Round-Tripping Foreign Direct Investment in the People's Republic of China: Scale, Causes and Implications', Asian Development Bank Institute Discussion Paper No. 7, June 2004.

Yongnian Zheng Minjia Chen, 'China's Recent SOE Reform and Its Social Consequences', China Policy Institute, University of Nottingham, Briefing Series – Issue 23, June 2007.

Young, Alwyn, 'Gold into Base Metals: Productivity Growth in the People's Republic of China During the Reform Period', NBER Working Paper No. 7856, August 2000.

Zhang, Wei, 'Why Is Foreign Investment Concentrated in the Coastal Areas?', *Harvard Asia Quarterly*, MA, Summer 2000.

Zheng, Wern & Tai You, 'China's Rise as a Manufacturing Powerhouse: Implications for Asia', MAS Staff Paper No. 42, Dec 2005.

Zheng, Yongnian and Chen, Minjia, 'China's Recent SOE Reform and Its Social Consequences', China Policy Institute, University of Nottingham, Briefing Series – Issue 23, June 2007.

NEWSPAPER/MAGAZINE/JOURNAL ARTICLES

Acharya, Shankar, 'Governance and Health', *Business Standard*, 30 August 2007.

Acharya, Shankar, 'Midsummer Madness?', 9 August 2007, *Business Standard*.

Aiyar, Pallavi, 'Agriculture: Where India and China Stand', *The Hindu*, 3 September 2007.

Altbach, Philip G., 'Tiny at the Top', *Wilson Quarterly*, Autumn 2006.

Anderlini, Jamil, 'China's State Sector Urged to Boost Economy', *Financial Times*, 26 December 2008.

Anderson, Jonathan, 'China Should Speed Up the Yuan's Rise', *The Far Eastern Economic Review*, July/August 2007.

Basant, Rakesh & Sebastian Morris, 'Competition Policy in India: Issues for a Globalising Economy', *Economic and Political Weekly*, 29 July 2000.

Behera, Laxman Kumar, 'China's Defence White Paper: Can India Draw Some Lessons?', *IDSA Strategic Comments*, www.idsa.in, 31 January 2007.

Behera, Laxman Kumar, 'Indian Defence Acquisition: Time for Change', *IDSA Strategic Comments*, www.idsa.in, 3 August 2007.

Behera, Laxman Kumar, 'The Indian Defence Budget 2007–08', *IDSA Strategic Comments*, www.idsa.in, 9 March 2007.

Bhalla, Surjit, 'How India is Different from China: It Doesn't Matter', *Business Standard*, 18 August 2007.

Bhalla, Surjit, 'Rupee, Self-Interest and RBI Policy', *Business Standard*, 29 September 2007.

Bremmer, Ian and Nouriel Roubini, 'Expect the World Economy to Suffer Through 2009', *The Wall Street Journal*, 23 January 2009.

Chaudhuri, Pramit Pal, 'India's Hydrocarbon Future', *Far Eastern Economic Review*, September 2007.

Cui, Li, 'China's Growing External Dependence', *Finance and Development*, IMF, Volume 44, Number 3, September 2007.

Daulet Singh, Zorawar, 'India's Rising Power: Myth or Reality?', World Affairs, Vol. 11, No. 4, Winter 2007.

Daulet Singh, Zorawar, 'Resurgence of Russia: Commercial realism can benefit India', *The Tribune*, 6 February 2007.

Daulet Singh, Zorawar, 'Security: India Loses Its Grip', *Asiatimes online*, 21 December 2006.

Deputy Direct of SASAC: 'China Will Actively Promote the Reform of Personnel System in SOE', *Xinhua* news, 25 October 2006.

Desai, Meghnad, 'India and China: An Essay in Comparative Political Economy', 31 March 2003.

Dickie, Mure, 'China unveils state aircraft builder', *Financial Times*, 12 May 2008.

Downs, Erica, 'China's Quest for Overseas Oil', *Far Eastern Economic Review*, September 2007.

Economics Focus, 'An Old Chinese Myth', *The Economist*, 3 January 2008.

Editorial, 'Assembly in China Vital for Sales, Says Airbus', *Financial Times*, 6 September 2007.

Editorial, 'China and the Future of the World', 28–29 April 2006, 'China's Future in the Age of Globalization', 29 April, *Panel Discussion*, http://chicagosociety.uchicago.edu/china

Editorial, 'China Expected to Overtake US to Become World's Second Largest Exporter', *People's Daily Online*, 21 August 2007.

Editorial, 'China Hopes a Homegrown Regional Jetliner Can Challenge Airbus and Boeing', *International Herald Tribune*, 7 September 2007.

Editorial, 'China Moves from Gatherer to Hunter', *Financial Times*, 22 August 2007.

Editorial, 'China Needs Innovation, OECD Says', *International Herald Tribune*, 27 August 2007.

Editorial, 'China Passes Antitrust Law, to Scrutinize More Deals', www.bloomberg.com, 30 August 2007.

Editorial, 'China Unveils Fund to Invest Forex Reserves', *Financial Times*, 29 September 2007.

Editorial, 'China, Singapore Agree to Further Economic Cooperation', *Xinhua*, 11 July 2007.

Editorial, 'China's Export of Electronic Info Products Up 26.2%', *China Daily*, 2 October 2007.

Editorial, 'China's Investment: Dim Sums', *The Economist*, 2 November 2006.

Editorial, 'Chinese Central SOEs Return 17 Bln Yuan from 2006 Profits', *Xinhua news*, 20 September 2007.

Editorial, 'Chinese Premier Says China-S. Korea Trade Cooperation Brings About Tangible Benefits', People's Daily Online, 11 April 2007.

Editorial, 'IEA Warns of "Supply Crunch" in Oil Despite High Prices', *International Herald Tribune*, 9 July 2007.

Editorial, 'India Inc. Facing Skilled Manpower Shortage: Survey', *Hindustan Times*, 8 July 2007.

Editorial, 'India Plans New Panel to look into Corporate M&As', *Reuters*, 29 August 2007.

Editorial, 'India Turns Focus on China in "Look East" Policy', *The Hindu*, 15 September 2007

Editorial, 'India's RBI Says More Infrastructure Spend, Farm Output Needed to Sustain Growth', www.forbes.com, 30 August 2007.

Editorial, 'Intel Breaks Ground in China for US$ 2.5 Billion Silicon Fabrication Plant', *International Herald Tribune*, 8 September 2007.

Editorial, 'KPMG: India Has to Pump $10 Billion in Energy Sector', *Deccan Chronicle*, 4 April 2006.

Editorial, 'Oil Import Bill Jumps to $40 b in April', www.sify.com, 10 April 2006.

Editorial, 'PetroChina to Buy Up to A$60 Billion of Australia LNG', www.bloomberg.com, 6 September 2007.

Editorial, 'Push for Power Reforms', *Tribune News Service*, www.tribuneindia.com, 26 February 2005.

Editorial, 'SASAC Sets Rigid Target for Central SOEs', *China Daily*, 30 August 2007.

Editorial, 'Sino-Indian Ties Cemented', *People's Daily Online*, 15 January 2008.

Editorial, 'The Drivers of Trade and Integration in Asia', Asian Development Outlook 2006, Asian Development Bank.

Editorial, 'Three Asian Giants', *The Economist*, 6 September 2007.

Editorial, 'Top 500 Enterprises 2007 Take Up 84 Percent of GDP', *China Daily*, 1 September 2007.

Editorial, 'U.S. Economic Slowdown Will Not Curb China's Growth', www.ResourceInvestor.com, 26 November 2006.

Editorial, 'Wen Calls for Further Development of China–Japan Trade, Economic Ties', *Xinhua news*, 12 April 2007.

Erskine, Alex, 'The Rise in China's FDI: Myths and Realities', Australia–China Free Trade Agreement Conference, Sydney, 12–13 August 2004, www.apec.org.

Ferguson, Niall, 'The Age of Obligation', *Financial Times*, 19 December 2008.

Ferguson, Niall, 'An Imaginary Retrospective of 2009', *Financial Times*, 15 December 2009.

'Global Job Losses "Could Hit 51m"', BBC News, http://news.bbc.co.uk, 28 January 2009.

Guruswamy, Mohan and Ronald Joseph Abraham, 'Redefining Poverty: A New Poverty Line for a New India', Centre for Policy Alternatives, New Delhi, February 2006, (Access report at http://cpasindia.org/reports/16-redefining-poverty-line-india.pdf).

Hofman, Bert and Kuijs, Louis, 'Profits Drive China's Boom', *Far Eastern Economic Review*, October 2006.

Hogg, Chris, 'Chinese Migrant Job Losses Mount', http://news.bbc.co.uk, 2 February 2009.

Jae-kyoung, Kim, 'Korea Braces for China Shock', www.koreatimes.co.kr, 27 January 2009.

Kapur, Devesh and Sunil Khilnani, 'Primary Concerns', *Hindustan Times*, 23 April 2006.

Kauper, Thomas E., 'Merger Control in the United States and the European Union: Some Observations', St. Johns Law Review; Spring 2000; 74; 2.

Lee, Amy, 'Soaring Salaries to Hit India IT Margins', *Financial Times*, 12 September 2007.

Lynn, Barry, 'Wake Up to the Old-Fashioned Power of the New Oligopolies', *Financial Times*, 15 February 2006.

Maddison, Angus, 'The World Economy: A Millennial Perspective', OECD Development Centre Studies, 2001.

Maddison, Angus, 'World Population, GDP and Per Capita GDP, 1-2003 AD', November 2006; For a critique of Maddison's estimates, see Bryan Haig's review of his *The World Economy: Historical Statistics* (OECD, 2003) in *The Economic Record*, Vol. 81 No. 252 (March 2005), pp. 91–93.

Maitra, Ramtanu, 'Why India's Economy Lags Behind China's', *Asiatimes*, 27 June 2003.

Malik, Rajeev, 'India's Handling of Rupee Remains a Riddle', www.rediff.com.

McDonnell, Brett H, Daniel A Farber, 'Are Efficient Antitrust Rules always Optimal?', Antitrust Bulletin, New York: Vol.48, Iss. 3; pg. 807, 29 pgs, Fall 2003.

Meyer, Henry and Ayesha Daya, 'Roubini Predicts U.S. Losses May Reach $3.6 Trillion', www.bloomberg.com, 20 Jan 2009.

Minda, Gary, 'Antitrust Regulability and the New Digital Economy: A Proposal for Integrating "Hard" and "Soft" Regulation', Antitrust Bulletin, New York, Vol. 46, Iss. 3; pp. 439, 73 pgs, Fall 2001.

Montek, Ahluwalia, 'India is "the" Destination for Investment', High Commission of India, London http://hcilondon.net.

Mukherjee, Andy, 'Asia Will Lose as "Made in China" Goes Local', www.bloomberg.com, 18 September 2007.

Mukherjee, Andy, 'India's Young Savers Will Prove McKinsey Wrong', www.bloomberg.com, 7 May 2007.

Mukherjee, Pranab, P. S. Suryanarayana, 'Strategic Partnership with China Will Mature', *The Hindu*, 18 September 2007.

Mukherji, Rahul, 'Managing Competition: Politics and the Building of Independent Regulatory Institutions', *India Review*, Vol. 2, No. 4, October 2004.

Nagaraj R., 'Industrial Growth in China and India: A Preliminary Comparison', *Economic and Political Weekly*, 21 May 2005.

OECD press release, 'China Will Become the World's Second Highest Investor in R&D by End of 2006, Finds OECD', www.oecd.org, 4 Dec 2006.

Oster, Shai, 'In China, a Domestic Shift Spurs New Approach on Natural Gas', *The Wall Street Journal*, 10 September 2007.

Pfaff, William, 'China: The Pretend Superpower', *International Herald Tribune*, 24 August 2007

Ram, Mohan T., 'Are FDI Flows into India for Real?', *The Economic Times*, 4 October 2007.

Rampilla, Narayana Rao, 'A Developing Judicial Perspective to India's Monopolies and Restrictive Trade Practices Act of 1969', *Antitrust Bulletin*, New York: Vol. 34, Iss. 3, Fall 1989.

Roach, Stephen, 'Global: China's Heavy Lifting', Morgan Stanley *Global Economic Forum*, March 2002.

'SASAC: The State-Owned Economy Should Maintain Absolute Control in Seven Sectors', *Xinhua* news, 19 December 2006.

Segal, Gerald, 'Does China Matter?', *Foreign Affairs*, September/October 1999.

Shourie, Arun, 'To Race China, First Let's Get Our Feet off the Brakes', *Indian Express*, 7 November 2006.

Sindharh, Jaspal Singh, 'Energy: Confrontation or Cooperation?', SAISPHERE, Johns Hopkins University, 2006. [http://www.saisjhu.edu/pubaffairs/publications/saisphere/winter06/.]

Singh, Joginder, 'Where India Doesn't Shine', *The Pioneer*, 26 August 2007.

Singh, Nirvikar, 'The Services-Manufacturing Debate', *Financial Express*, 26 January 2006.

Singh, Nirvikar, 'The Ten Sectors that Need a Boost', *Financial Express*, 12 December 2006.

Subramanian, 'FDI: Any Lessons from China?', *The Hindu*, 18 November 2002.

Subramanian, Arvind, 'Precocious India', *Business Standard*, 14 August 2007.

Summers, Lawrence, 'Sovereign Funds Shake the Logic of Capitalism', *Financial Times*, 30 July 2007.

Thomas, Cherian, 'India Exports Fell in December for 3rd Straight Month', www.bloomberg.com, 2 February 2009.

Visaria, Leela and Pravin, 'Long-Term Population Projections for Major States, 1991–2101', *Economic & Political Weekly*, November 2003.

Wolf, Martin, 'The Right Way to Respond to China's Exploding Surplus', *Financial Times*, 30 May 2007.

Xinzhen, Lan, 'State Seeks Control of Critical Industries', www.beijingreview.com, 11 January 2007.

Yanping, Li, 'China Faces Worst Unemployment in Decades as Slowdown Deepens', www.bloomberg.com, 20 January 2009.

Yiwei, Wang, 'China's Rise: An unlikely Pillar of US Hegemony', *Harvard International Review*, 22 March 2007.

Zheng, Jinghai, Arne Bigsten and Angang Hu, 'Can China's Growth be Sustained?: A Productivity Perspective, for the Special Issue on Law, Finance, and Economic Growth in China', *World Development*, 2007.

LIST OF FREQUENTLY USED TERMS

Billion	One thousand million
BIMARU	The states of Bihar, Madhya Pradesh, Rajasthan and Uttar Pradesh
BRIC	The fast-growing developing economies of Brazil, Russia, India and China
Crore	Ten million (or one hundred lakhs)
DRDO	Defence Research and Development Organization
FAI	Fixed-asset investment
FDI	Foreign direct investment
HALE	Healthy life expectancy at birth
HDI	Human Development Index
ICOR	Incremental capital–output ratio
Lakh	One hundred thousand
LNG	Liquefied natural gas
NOC	National oil companies
OECD	Organization for Economic Cooperation and Development
PSU	Public sector units
SASAC	State-owned Assets Supervision and Administration Commission
SEZ	Special economic zones
SOE	State-owned enterprises
Trillion	One thousand billion

INDEX

Page numbers followed by a "t" or "c" indicate that the entry is included in a table or chart.